Praise for
DeMark Indicators
by Jason Perl

"Tom DeMark, the man whose work inspired this book, is a unique, interesting, and ofttimes iconoclastic technical analyst. Simply put, he thinks about the markets differently from the way you or I do. So why should you read this book? Because, having read it, you will almost certainly think about the markets and technical analysis differently."

—JOHN BOLLINGER, CFA, CMT, www.BollingerBands.com

"Jason Perl has taken the playbook from the market's John Wooden, Tom DeMark, and translated it engagingly in a format that traders of all levels will appreciate. As one who has used these indicators for more than twenty years, I too am appreciative of Jason's clarity."

—PETER BORISH, CHAIRMAN AND CEO, Computer Trading Corporation

"Jason Perl has created a trading primer that will help both the professional and the layman interpret the DeMark indicators, which I believe represent the most robust and powerful methods to track securities and establish timely investment positions. Think of *DeMark Indicators* as the Rosetta stone of market-timing technology."

—JOHN BURBANK, FOUNDER AND CIO, Passport Capital

"Having observed his market calls real time over the years, I can say that Jason Perl's application of the DeMark indicators distinguishes his work from industry peers when it comes to market timing. This book demonstrates how traders can benefit from his insight, using the studies to identify the exhaustion of established trends or the onset of new ones. Whether you're fundamentally or technically inclined, Perl's *DeMark Indicators* is an invaluable trading resource."

—LEON G. COOPERMAN, CHAIRMAN, Omega Advisors

"Jason Perl is the trader's technician. DeMark indicators are a difficult subject matter, but Jason shows simply how the theory can be applied practically to markets. Whether you're day-trading or taking medium-term positions, using the applications can only be of increased value."

—DAVID KYTE, FOUNDER, Kyte Group Limited

DeMARK
INDICATORS

Related titles also available from BLOOMBERG PRESS

Option Strategies for Directionless Markets
by Anthony J. Saliba with Joseph C. Corona and Karen E. Johnson

Trading Option Greeks
by Dan Passarelli

Breakthroughs in Technical Analysis
edited by David Keller

Trading ETFs
Gaining an Edge with Technical Analysis
by Deron Wagner

New Insights on Covered Call Writing
by Richard Lehman and Lawrence G. McMillan

New Thinking in Technical Analysis
edited by Rick Bensignor

———————————

A complete list of our titles is available at
www.bloomberg.com/books

Bloomberg MARKET ESSENTIALS
TECHNICAL ANALYSIS

DeMARK INDICATORS

Jason PERL

FOREWORD BY THOMAS R. DeMARK

BLOOMBERG PRESS

NEW YORK

First edition published 2008
3 5 7 9 10 8 6 4

Library of Congress Cataloging-in-Publication Data

Perl, Jason.
    DeMark indicators / Jason Perl; foreword by Thomas R. DeMark. — 1st ed.
       p. cm.
    Includes index.
    Summary: "Tom DeMark, creator of the widely known and respected DeMark indicators, served as mentor to author Jason Perl. Perl defines and explains how the indicators bring a successful trading decision to conclusion, and offers aggressive or conservative alternative indications. With a chart or graphic explaining each indicator and a foreword by Tom DeMark"—Provided by publisher.
    ISBN 978-1-57660-314-7
    1. Investment analysis.   2. Stock price forecasting.   3. Financial instruments—Prices—Forecasting.   I. Title.

HG4529.P475 2008
332.63'2042—dc22

                                                                        2008030305

Contents

Foreword

I REMEMBER AS if it were yesterday: It was the first seminar I had given in London in some time, and the weather was unseasonably cold for March. The forecast was for sleet and snow, and I expected it to have a dampening effect on attendance. I had flown almost twelve hours to get there, but I didn't mind the turn of events: I had been told to expect a large number of cash currency traders at the session, and, although I was actively involved in equities, commodities, and financial and currency futures, the cash currency market was a segment of the market I was not so well acquainted with. I arrived at the seminar, then, expecting to be speaking to only a handful of traders, but, much to my chagrin, not only was there already a large turnout, but there was also a large contingent of cash currency traders.

Just prior to the seminar, I had been introduced to a pleasant young man who actively followed the cash currency markets. Surprisingly, he also appeared to be well versed about many of my indicators. During my presentation, when the audience posed cash currency and indicator questions, he was prepared to answer them. His occasional observations interacted well with my presentation, and so I very much appreciated his contributions. That exchange served as the genesis of what was to become a long-term professional and personal friendship that endures to this day.

Little did I know on the day of the seminar that Jason Perl had only recently graduated from a prestigious English university and begun a currency consulting service. His deep knowledge of the markets and the indicators certainly impressed me, as well as the others in attendance, and made it appear that he was someone with much more experience. Not only did he hold his own with these professionals but seemed to me to be so knowledgeable that I frequently referred others to him. He was the only person I knew who was conversant in the cash currency markets who could apply my indicators to them effectively. Jason never let me down. The feedback I received from his clients was always very positive. I knew he enjoyed consulting, but, at the same time, I realized that he was destined for bigger and better professional challenges.

In 2000, Jason reported that he had accepted a position at a large investment bank. While I was happy for him, I was concerned that a large company might have a bureaucratic structure that would stifle Jason's professional career and growth. That, however, turned out not to be the case. It soon became apparent that any apprehension I had had was ill founded. Jason's skills transcended any corporate boundaries that may have existed. His knowledge of the indicators and their real-time application expanded beyond simply foreign currencies and extended quickly to other markets. This departure from his original job description was a clear indication that both his colleagues at the company and his corporate clients valued Jason's unique analytical abilities, and he was more than willing to oblige them. His rapid ascent up the corporate ladder is a testament to his tremendous grasp of the indicators and the markets and his tireless, dedicated work ethic.

What is truly commendable is that Jason's strong appetite for learning has always been aligned with his desire to teach and advise others. What is well known is the tremendous respect his clients and peers have for Jason as a market strategist, but what may be overlooked is the admiration that these same people have for Jason as a person. Far too often in the investment industry one takes for granted those who may have contributed to one's success. Whether it be a mentor or a fellow worker who directs one along the path to success or teaches the intricacies and meaningful aspects of the business, or the family who makes sacrifices that allow one to devote the time and energy required to be successful, one often has a tendency to forget the people who made contributions. Jason, however, is unlike others: He has not forgotten those who have contributed to his career, and what's more important is that he has graciously and willingly reciprocated by sharing the knowledge he has acquired with others. Not only clients, but also total strangers, have approached Jason, and he has spent time with them, assisting them with their trading.

Many years ago, when the DeMark indicators were first introduced onto the various data-service networks (among which was Bloomberg), the audience awareness of the indicators' construction and application was limited. I wrote a couple of books and articles at the time that included charts showing how they could be used. Since then, I have added some features to the indicators and expanded the indicator universe. It was time for a fresh perspective and updated charts. Other than my son, TJ, who was working full time for Steve Cohen at SAC Capital, the most likely person to take on the project was Jason. When we discussed the possibility of a new book, he was receptive to the idea, and I was confident his experience and active application of the studies to various markets would provide an excellent foundation for a new book.

Over the years, Jason has been a passionate missionary for the indicators, highlighting their value to central banks, large institutional and hedge funds and to other professionals within his large, worldwide company network. His knowledge of the market models is vast, he is current with the latest indicator upgrades, and he is sensitive to the questions users of different skill levels might have regarding the indicators' construction and application. What is most important is that he has profitably applied the indicators, and his advisory-service trading record has been exceptional. It made sense to me, and I was certain it would to readers as well: Jason was the right person at the right time to be the author of a book devoted to the indicators.

The question now was who would be the ideal publisher. There was no question in our minds that it would have to be Bloomberg. Bloomberg has programmed the indicators and has a large staff dedicated to ensuring that the indicators are updated and working properly. The application specialists are well versed in the indicators and well equipped to answer any questions clients might have. It was a perfect fit.

I am pleased to have Jason as author of a book that represents my career's research efforts. His command of the indicators is unparalleled, as is his ability to present the subject matter succinctly and clearly. His self-effacing nature conceals his many skills. What is remarkable about Jason is that, after all the success and fame he has achieved, he is still the same person I met many years ago on that cold wintry day. Thank you, and congratulations, Jason, for a job well done. At your young age, you have accomplished much, and I am certain more major milestones will follow.

TOM DEMARK

Acknowledgments

I AM GRATEFUL to my wife, Jennifer, for her love, patience, tolerance, support, and understanding at all times and in particular while I was writing this book.

To my parents for their love, guidance, and support over the years and for instilling in me a sense of what's right and for never giving up on me, even when they discovered I didn't want to be a lawyer or an accountant;

To Tom DeMark, my friend and mentor, whose ongoing commitment and enthusiasm for decoding markets is infectious;

To all the people at UBS: the management of UBS FICC, our FX salespeople, the Technical and Fundamental Strategy groups, the Web editors, and the Web development teams;

To Piers Fallowfield-Cooper, for believing in me and for giving me a chance at the start of my career;

To Ian and Honor Robertson, for encouraging continuous self-improvement and for facilitating my first meeting with Tom DeMark;

To the management and staff of Bloomberg, CQG, and eSignal, for being so responsive over the years to my requirements as a demanding customer;

To Philip Algar, Taso Anastasiou, Rick Bensignor, Roderick Bentley, Peter Borish, John Burbank III, Antonio Carbone, Gerald Chan, Jim Chorek, Kevan Conlon, Leon Cooperman, Darren Coote, Herbert Coyne, Tom DeMark Jr., Steve Einhorn, Cheryl Galante, Laurie Goodman, Laeeth Isharc, Andrew Joncus, Dave Keller, Rick Knox,

David Kyte, James Loh, Ger-Ghee Low, Martin Masterson, Tim McCullough, Mansoor Mohi-uddin, Todd Morakis, David Munro, Herwig Prielipp, Guido Riolo, Joseph Schroeter, Guy Scott, Fabian Shey, Joe Sigelman, Ed Solari, Eugene Sorenson, Reto Stadelman, Mark Steinert, Steven Stewart, Matt Storz, Glen Sulam, Anthony Tan, Gregg Tan, Doug Tengler, David Toth, Ron William, Larry Williams, David Wood, Stan Yabroff, and to all the numerous clients of UBS for their interest in and support of my work over the years.

And finally, many thanks to my editors; Ronnie McDavid for her patience and tolerance and for not suggesting I look up the meaning of the words "and finally," and to David George, for instilling in me that a picture is only worth a thousand words when it's correctly annotated.

Introduction

IN THE EARLY 1990S, while studying economics, I was working as a summer intern at the Bank of England, in their Gilt-Edged and Money Markets Division. One day, in September of 1990, just before the release of the U.K.'s August inflation number, a colleague and I happened to be working in a room with no access to outside communication. My colleague asked me to speculate on what I thought the inflation number would be, and I gave him my best educated guess.

"I think you will be surprised to find that it will actually be much higher," my colleague told me. "On that basis," he asked, "how do you think the market will react?"

Summoning all the theoretical knowledge I could muster, I outlined a textbook case, giving the expected implications for the pound sterling and for gilts.

As it turned out, although my colleague was right about the inflation number, I was completely wrong about the market's reaction. Perception can often be very different from reality; this was not only an epiphany for me on positioning, but also an event that shook my confidence. *If I can't even get it right when I have the information at my disposal in advance,* I thought, *what hope will I have when I have no advance knowledge and am left to fend for myself?*

Fast forward two years: I had just graduated from university, the U.K. was in a recession, and I was one of thousands of unemployed finance majors struggling to find a job. If I was really intent on working in the financial markets, someone suggested, the best thing I might do would be to learn technical analysis—the study of historical price charts and market timing. Technical analysis was a new, but promising, strategy in Europe at that time, but it might be an area where I could create a niche for myself.

That turned out to be good advice. Then, being something of a contrarian by nature, I was drawn to a contrarian approach, and, in my research, one name I was coming across again and again was that of Tom DeMark. He had just written *The New Science of Technical Analysis,* and he impressed me as being a particularly original thinker.

One day my friend Ian Robertson, knowing I had been studying DeMark's work for a while, asked if I'd be interested in attending a seminar DeMark was giving in London. I jumped at the chance, but, when I went to the seminar, I was more than a little humbled to discover that, after me, the most junior person in the audience of twenty was the global head of fixed income at a large American investment bank.

After the session, I managed to chat briefly with Tom, and he even promised to call me when he got back to the United States. Since the United States was a long way away, however, and I had only scrawled my phone number on the back of a borrowed business card, it seemed highly unlikely that I would ever hear from him again. Therefore, one Sunday morning some weeks later (at 4:30 a.m. London time, to be precise), I was not expecting the phone call that woke me from a sound sleep.

"This is Tom DeMark," said the voice on the phone. "We spoke a few months ago. You had some questions about my indicators?" (For someone with such a good sense of market timing, Tom had a surprisingly bad sense of time zone differences.)

In my foggy state, I abruptly asked him to call back later—but didn't think of asking for a call-back number. Not a smart response from a young man who was unemployed. To my good fortune and to Tom's credit, however, he did ring back later that morning, and after that call we eventually began to have regular discussions on the markets.

One particular day, about a year later, when we were speaking, Tom complimented me on a particularly good currency call: "Well done," he said. "You must have made a fortune today."

"Well, not exactly," I replied, and confessed that I was still working from my bedroom at my parents' house, using a charting system

I had bartered for the use of, in exchange for some consulting work I had done, and I had not had a lot riding on my clever currency call.

There was silence, as Tom digested the information that he had been wasting a good deal of his time during the past year in talking to an unemployed student. "Well," he responded, more kindly than I expected, "why don't you go and work for a hedge fund?" and proceeded to give me the names of ten major traders who, at one time or another, had offered him money-management or employment opportunities and who (if I mentioned his name) might just be hot contacts for me. On a more sober note, he added, "You might be a decent analyst, but being effective on the job also means being able to sell yourself. This will be a good test."

The rest, as they say, is history, and I've not looked back since. I know that those people who are new to Tom's work often question his motives for sharing his ideas, but I've always been grateful to him for kick starting my career when I had nothing more to offer than a keen interest in markets and youthful enthusiasm for his indicators. He has selflessly introduced me to many of the market greats, and never, in all the fourteen years I've known him, has he ever asked for anything in return.

Tom's indicators have enabled me to make some very good market calls. While it's tough employing a contrarian methodology, I hope those who have followed my calls over the years have come to realize that it is not entirely by chance that there have been more good calls than bad ones. This book has been written because clients around the world have asked me to provide them with a detailed explanation of the DeMark indicators.

There are some who might question whether the validity of Tom's work will diminish over time, as more people become familiar with it. In response, I'd urge those people to think about dieting. Since the solution is simple—eat less and exercise more—why is the diet business a multibillion-dollar industry?

The answer is that people don't like to acknowledge that the solution is a simple one, that it comes down to discipline. The truth—that even if you have a diet plan, it won't be effective unless you stick with the program—is the same for the DeMark indicators. Discipline with the DeMark indicators is perhaps even more difficult than dieting, because, when the trend is going against you, there's always a temptation to abandon the indicators. As with dieting, applying the indicators is a strategy that has its ups and downs, but, as I think you'll see from the following chapters, using the indicators provides an edge in terms of acute risk/reward trading opportunities and market timing. If you have the patience and discipline to persevere with them, the indicators will produce positive results over time.

I will walk you through the signature DeMark countertrend studies like TD Sequential™ and TD Combo™, but I'll also discuss many of Tom's other indicators that offer an objective spin on more conventional techniques, such as moving averages, momentum oscillators, trendlines, retracements, and Elliott wave. (An index of all the indicators, listing the pages where they are described, can be found at the back of the book.)

Some have questioned whether the widespread acceptance of the DeMark indicators might diminish their effectiveness. For those people, I return to the food metaphor. Look at world-renowned chef Gordon Ramsay: He might have sold a lot of cookbooks, but his book sales have proved no threat to his restaurants.

Still, the real-time application of Tom's indicators is by no means easy. There are no get-rich-quick shortcuts. You must work hard and be disciplined, objective, and dispassionate about the signals they generate. You must adhere rigidly to strict money-management rules. I am merely supplying you with some good tried-and-tested recipes; it's up to you to do the cooking.

Author's Note

THE DEMARK INDICATORS are available on Aspen Graphics, Bloomberg, CQG, Thomson Financial, and TradeStation. For cash foreign exchange markets, 10:00 p.m. local London time has been used as the close for the global trading day. For simplicity, most of the charts in this book are daily price charts, but since these studies are based on relative price action, they can all be applied to any market or time frame.

Also, unless noted otherwise, all charts have been taken from the Bloomberg Professional service.

About DeMark Indicator Trademarks

ALL DeMARK INDICATORS listed here are registered trademarks and are protected by U.S. trademark law. Any unauthorized use without the express written permission of Market Studies or Thomas DeMark is a violation of the law. The indicators are as follows:

TD Setup™, TD Setup Trend™ (TDST™), TD Countdown™, TD Sequential™, TD Combo™, TD Aggressive Sequential™, TD Aggressive Combo™, TD Camouflage™, TD Clop™, TD Clopwin™, TD Open™, TD Trap™, TD Termination Count™, TD Reference Close™, TD D-Wave™, TD Demand Line™, TD Supply Line™, TD Relative Retracement™, TD Absolute Retracement™, TD Retracement Arc™, TD Trend Factor™, TD Propulsion™, TD Range Expansion Index™ (TD REI™), TD Price Oscillator Qualifier™ (TD POQ™), TD DeMarker 1™, TD DeMarker 2™, TD Pressure™, TD Rate of Change™ (TD ROC™), TD Alignment™, TD Moving Average 1™, TD Moving Average 2™, TD Range Projection™, TD Range Expansion Breakout™ (TD REBO™), TD Channel One™, TD Channel Two™, TD Differential™, TD Reverse Differential™, TD Anti-Differential™, and TD Waldo Patterns™.

CHAPTER 1

TD Sequential
Defining the Trend and Identifying Exhaustion Points

WHEN I STARTED LOOKING at the DeMark indicators in the early 1990s, it was TD Sequential that first piqued my interest. I had previously come across other technical studies that identified trading opportunities well when prices were trending, and still other indicators that were particularly suited to ranges, but I had found it frustrating that none of these approaches was sufficiently dynamic to distinguish between these two very different types of price action.

TD Sequential appeals to me because it addresses that problem, having both momentum (TD Setup) and trending (TD Countdown) components. Furthermore, it's completely objective and incorporates disciplined money-management rules, and (because it's based on relative price action) you can apply it to any market or time frame, regardless of the market's underlying volatility, without having to change any of the default indicator settings.

For those of us brought up in the computer age, it may seem hard to believe, but Tom DeMark developed TD Sequential by hand, through a process of trial and error, in the 1970s. It never ceases to amaze me how something originally created to analyze daily price data can be applied so effectively, more than thirty years later, to any time frame—from one minute to one year—and to any market.

Since the majority of people are trend followers, it's hardly surprising that "the trend is your friend" is one of the most widely quoted trading mantras. While it may seem counterintuitive, given that most people do follow trends, TD Sequential attempts to isolate prospective exhaustion points in ranges, to anticipate market tops and bottoms when it believes prices are overbought or oversold and during trends when sentiment is invariably at an extreme. Even if you are not inclined to the technical, TD Sequential can be helpful for market-timing purposes, as an adjunct to your existing arsenal of trading tools. Traders oriented to fundamentals tell me it helps them determine take-profit levels when they would otherwise be reliant on a less-efficient price-reversal pattern to close out a profitable position. TD Sequential also highlights, at the time the signal is generated, points where one should refrain from establishing or adding to an existing position in the direction of the underlying trend. Once you're comfortable with the methodology, however, you can use TD Sequential as I do, to fade trends.

Let's look at the components of TD Sequential in order to understand how and why it manages to be so versatile. The indicator has two components: TD Setup, which relies on momentum to define price ranges, and TD Countdown, which is trend based, and looks for low-risk opportunities to fade established directional moves. As TD Sequential is probably the most-talked-about TD indicator, I'll explain it in detail for both bullish and bearish scenarios, as well as answer some frequently asked questions.

TD Setup

TD Setup is one component of TD Sequential; the other component, TD Countdown, cannot come into play until a TD Setup formation is complete. TD Setup, however, is not only a prerequisite for the broader-trend-reversal TD Countdown signal; it is also an indicator, one that can help determine whether a market is likely to be confined to a trading range or starting a directional trend. TD Setup, of course, has both buy and sell indicators, and I will address them separately.

The prerequisite for a TD Buy Setup is a Bearish TD Price Flip, which indicates a switch from positive to negative momentum (**Figure 1.1**).

■ **Bearish TD Price Flip**

A Bearish TD Price Flip occurs when the market records a close *greater than* the close four bars earlier, immediately followed by a close *less than* the close four bars earlier.

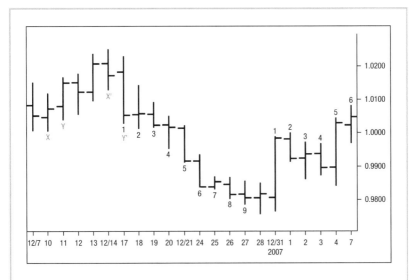

FIGURE 1.1   **Bearish TD Price Flip to Initiate a TD Buy Setup**

The chart of USDCAD illustrates the price action necessary to produce a bearish TD Price Flip for the initiation of a TD Buy Setup, that is, a close *greater than* the close four price bars earlier, immediately followed by a close *less than* the close four bars earlier. In this instance, the close of X' is above the close of X, and X' is followed by Y', which is below Y. The chart also shows the extension of that price action into an uninterrupted series of nine consecutive closes, each one less than the corresponding close four price bars earlier.

Note: The bar on which the bearish TD Price Flip occurs qualifies as bar one of the prospective TD Buy Setup.

TD Buy Setup

After a bearish TD Price Flip, there must be nine consecutive closes, each one less than the corresponding close four bars earlier.

Since the indicator was originally designed to look at daily price data, a comparison of the closing price with the closing price four bars earlier represents a rolling week.

Interruption of a TD Buy Setup

If, at any point, the sequence—of nine consecutive closing prices less than the closing price four bars earlier (up to and including the close of TD Buy Setup bar nine)—is interrupted, the developing TD Buy Setup will be canceled and must begin anew.

Having to start all over again can test one's patience, because it postpones the appearance of a signal. But the delay is meaningful, because it suggests a change in market dynamics, which the indicator acknowledges by changing its behavior.

Completion of the First Phase of TD Sequential

Once a TD Buy Setup successfully reaches nine, the first phase of TD Sequential is complete, and a TD Buy Countdown can begin.

TD Sell Setup

For a prospective sell situation, before a TD Sell Countdown can begin, we need to see a bullish TD Price Flip—a switch from negative to positive momentum (**Figure 1.2**)—in order to initiate a TD Sell Setup.

▪ Bullish TD Price Flip

A Bullish TD Price Flip occurs when the market records a close *less than* the close four bars before, immediately followed by a close *greater than* the close four bars earlier.

Once the bullish TD Price Flip occurs, a TD Sell Setup can begin.

▪ TD Sell Setup

Once the bullish TD Price Flip occurs, a TD Sell Setup, consisting of nine consecutive closes, each one *greater than* the corresponding close four bars earlier, can begin.

▪ Interruption of a TD Sell Setup

If

At any point, the sequence of nine consecutive closes *greater than* the close four bars earlier is interrupted—up to and including the close of TD Buy Setup bar nine—

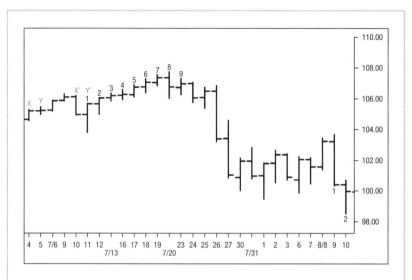

FIGURE 1.2   Bullish TD Price Flip to Initiate a TD Sell Setup

The chart of AUDJPY illustrates the price action necessary to produce a bullish TD Price
Flip for the initiation of a TD Sell Setup, that is, a close *less than* the close four price bars
earlier, immediately followed by a close *greater than* the close four bars earlier. In this
instance, the close of X' is below the close of X, and X' is followed by Y', which is above Y.
The chart also shows the extension of that price action into an uninterrupted series of nine
consecutive closes, each one greater than the corresponding close four price bars earlier.

*Note: The bar on which the TD Price Flip occurs qualifies as bar one of the prospective TD Buy
Setup.*

Then

The developing TD Buy Setup will be canceled and must begin anew.

*After a TD Sell Setup successfully reaches nine, the first phase of TD
Sequential is complete, and a TD Sell Countdown can begin.*

Using TDST Levels to Determine the Underlying Trend Bias

Many people move straight from TD Setup to TD Countdown, overlook-
ing the implications of a completed TD Setup. But, in doing so, they miss
the valuable directional insight provided by this aspect of TD Sequential.

Since it compares the current close with the corresponding close four bars earlier, TD Setup has a momentum component, but, unlike more conventional momentum indicators, TD Setup is dynamic. This is an important distinction that enables TD Setup to differentiate between trending and nontrending price action. Each time the market completes a TD Setup, the true price extreme of that move—known as the TD Setup Trend (TDST)—redefines the range in terms of price levels. From a TD perspective, the ensuing price response to that TD Setup Trend level helps to determine the underlying directional bias.

TD Sequential vs. More Conventional Momentum Indicators

Conventional momentum indicators, such as the RSI (Relative Strength Index), are typically calibrated between zero and one hundred, and have the constraint of fixed overbought and oversold zones, which makes them less reliable when price action switches between ranges and trends. In a strongly directional up move, the RSI rarely pulls back into extreme oversold territory (which is typically set around twenty-five), but, instead, finds support between an oscillator reading of fifty and forty.

Similarly, in a strongly directional down move, the RSI tends not to retrace into extreme overbought territory (typically set around seventy-five). Instead, the RSI usually finds resistance in the oscillator zone between fifty and sixty.

The TD Setup indicator, on the other hand, adjusts dynamically, in line with the price action, since it recalculates what it considers to be range extremes in the form of TDST Levels every time a new TD Setup completes. See **Figures 1.3** and **1.4**.

■ TD Setup Scenario I: Consolidation/Reversal

If

A price fails to record a close beyond the absolute high or low of the most recently completed TD Setup in the opposite direction—that is, the TDST Level—up to and including the completion of bar nine of the current active TD Setup,

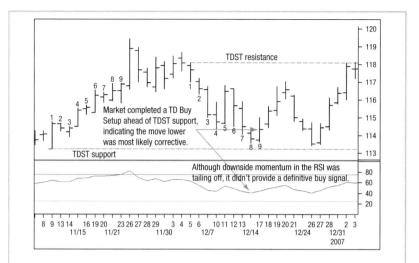

FIGURE 1.3 **Scenario 1: Consolidation/Reversal**

In the chart of the U.S. 30-year bond (USH8), although the RSI never enters oversold territory, there is a clear signal to enter longs upon completion of the TD Buy Setup—that is, the close of TD Buy Setup bar nine—because none of the bars within the TD Buy Setup phase has sufficient momentum to close below TDST support.

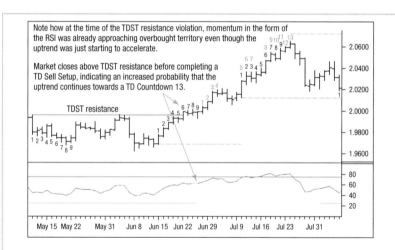

FIGURE 1.4 **Scenario 2: Trend Extension**

In the chart of GBPUSD, when the market closes above TDST resistance, it suggests there is a heightened risk that the developing bull trend will remain intact and price action will most likely continue to extend higher.

Note: At the time of the TDST break, the RSI is already approaching overbought territory, even though the uptrend is only beginning to accelerate.

Then

The market is deemed to have insufficient momentum to break out of the range.

Prices should then experience a short-term reversal of the underlying trend, or at least a consolidation, lasting a minimum of one to four price bars.

It is not significant if the TDST Level is violated on an intrabar basis; what is relevant is only whether or not the market is able to sustain a TDST break on a closing basis (**Figures 1.5** and **1.6**).

■ TD Setup Scenario II: Confirmed Trend Extension

If

Price exceeds the extreme absolute high or low of a previous TD Setup in the opposite direction on a closing basis,

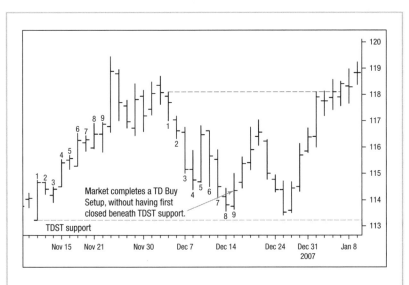

FIGURE 1.5   **TD Buy Setup Unable to Close Below TDST Support**

The chart of the March U.S. 30-year bond (USH8) shows a TD Buy Setup unable to close below TDST support, indicating that buying pressure remains the dominant force, with the market therefore likely to recover near term, since it has insufficient downward momentum to stage a breakout of the range to the downside.

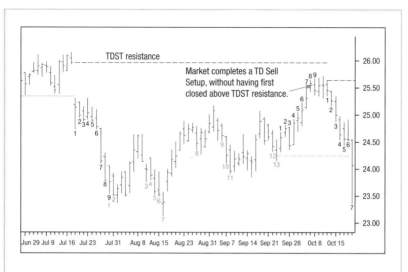

FIGURE 1.6   **TD Sell Setup Unable to Close Above TDST Resistance**

The chart of Pfizer shows a TD Sell Setup unable to close above TDST resistance, indicating that selling pressure remains the dominant force, with the market therefore vulnerable to a short-term correction, since it has insufficient upward momentum to break out of the range to the upside.

Then

The market is deemed to have sufficient momentum to facilitate a sustained break out of the range.

Prices should then continue in the direction of the underlying trend, and quite possibly move toward a completed TD Countdown before a reversal occurs.

From personal experience, I find that, if a TDST level breaks up to and including bar three of a prospective TD Setup, there is a good chance that the market will continue in the direction of the break, at least until the completion of the developing TD Setup (**Figures** 1.3, 1.4, **1.7**, and **1.8**).

TD Buy Setup "Perfection"

TD Buy Setup "perfection" is the prerequisite for entering a long position based on a completed TD Buy Setup.

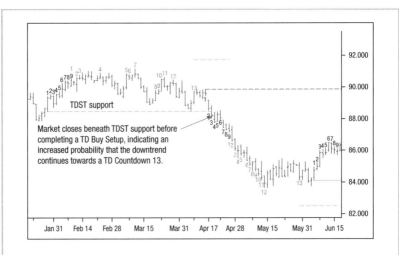

FIGURE 1.7   **Market Close Below TDST Support Prior to the Completion of a TD Buy Setup**

In the chart of the USD Index (DXY), the market closes below TDST support prior to the completion of a TD Buy Setup, indicating that selling pressure has intensified, with the market having sufficient bearish momentum to sustain a break to the downside.

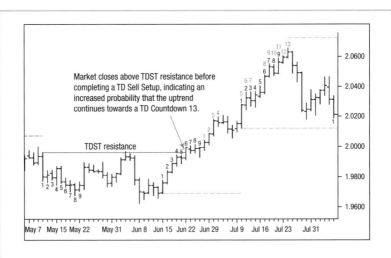

FIGURE 1.8   **Market Close Above TDST Resistance After Initial Rebuff**

In the chart of GBPUSD, the market, having initially been rebuffed by TDST resistance, subsequently closes above resistance prior to the completion of a TD Sell Setup, indicating that buying pressure has intensified and the market has sufficient bullish momentum to sustain a break to the upside.

■ TD Buy Setup "Perfection"

The low of bars eight or nine of the TD Buy Setup or a subsequent low must be less than, or equal to, the lows of bars six and seven of the TD Buy Setup.

TD Setup perfection is deferred until that happens, and, as long as that situation remains, the risk exists for a retest of the price low of TD Buy Setup bars six or seven, prior to the minimally expected response of a one- to four-bar consolidation/reversal. Before the trader enters a long position based on a completed TD Buy Setup, TD Buy Setup perfection is needed to increase the probability of his entering the market at or near an interim price low.

Note: Perfected TD Setups (**Figure 1.9**) can be seen by checking the TD Setup perfection arrows under the TD Sequential Setup "properties" on the Bloomberg terminal toolbar.

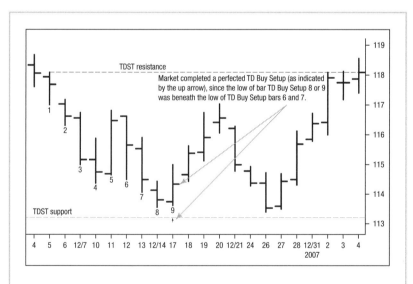

FIGURE 1.9 **Perfected TD Buy Setup**

In the chart of the U.S. 30-year bond (USH8), the market records a perfected TD Buy Setup bar nine, since the lows of TD Setup bars eight or nine are less than the lows of TD Setup bars six and seven.

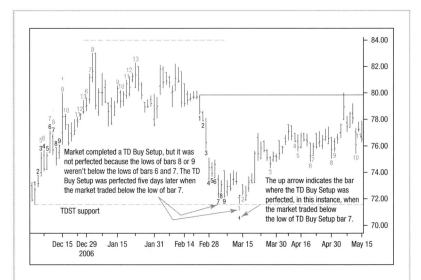

FIGURE 1.10   **Unperfected TD Buy Setup**

In the chart of Hutchison Whampoa, the market reaches TD Buy Setup bar nine, but the TD Buy Setup is not perfected because the lows of TD Buy Setup bars eight or nine are not less than the lows of TD Buy Setup bars six and seven. This pattern shows an increased risk that the market could come back to retest the lesser of bars six and seven before the expected consolidation/reversal materializes. The consolidation/reversal does come, five days later, and the up arrow below the bar indicates where the TD Buy Setup is eventually perfected.

The absence of TD Buy Setup perfection (**Figure 1.10**) doesn't *retard* the onset of a TD Buy Countdown, but it is an important consideration for those who want to trade TD Buy Setups.

Trading a TD Buy Setup

Other than saying that one can *initiate* a position if a TD Buy Setup holds TDST support on a closing basis, DeMark doesn't go into detail about how a trader can actually define the parameters for such a signal. Here is how *I* think TD Buy Setups (**Figure 1.11**) can be traded objectively, using a very clear set of rules:

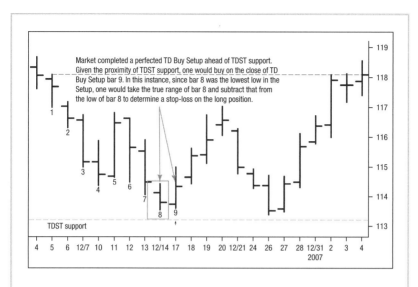

FIGURE 1.11 **Trading a Perfected TD Buy Setup**

In the chart of the U.S. 30-year bond (USH8), the market records a perfected TD Buy Setup ahead of TDST support.

Perl's Rules for Trading TD Buy Setups Objectively

Many people believe, mistakenly, that one should initiate a long position following every completed TD Buy Setup. I advise against doing that except under the following conditions:

1. When the TD Buy Setup has been perfected, that is, the low of TD Buy Setup bar eight or nine is less than the lows of TD Buy Setup bars six and seven,

2. When none of the bars within the TD Buy Setup has closed below TDST support, and

3. When the close of TD Buy Setup bar nine is in close proximity to TDST support.

I also prefer the close of TD Buy Setup bar nine to be less than the close of TD Buy Setup bar eight, but this is optional.

▪ Risk Management: Calculating the TD Risk Level for Trading a TD Buy Setup

1. Identify the TD Buy Setup bar with the lowest true low, and

2. Subtract the true range of that bar from its true low. (For example, if TD Buy Setup bar eight has the lowest true low, subtract the true range of that bar from its true low.)

The expectation would be for a return toward the upper-range extreme, as defined by TDST Resistance, in other words, the true high of the most recently completed TD Buy Setup. Typically, I would take the trade only if the difference between the entry price (close of TD Buy Setup bar nine), and TDST Resistance is more than 1.5 times the difference between the close of TD Buy Setup bar nine and the TD risk level.

▪ TD Sell Setup "Perfection"

The high of TD Sell Setup bars eight or nine or a subsequent high must be greater than, or equal to, the highs of TD Sell Setup bars six and seven.

TD Sell Setup perfection is deferred until that happens, and, as long as that situation exists, the risk is for a retest of the price high of bars six or seven, prior to the expected minimal response of a one- to four-bar consolidation/reversal.

The absence of TD Sell Setup perfection doesn't *retard* the onset of a TD Sell Countdown, but it is an important consideration for those who want to trade TD Sell Setups. To increase the probability of entering the market at or near an interim price high, traders should wait for a TD Sell Setup to be perfected before entering a short position based on a completed TD Sell Setup (**Figures 1.12** and **1.13**).

Trading a TD Sell Setup

As with the TD Buy Setups, DeMark doesn't describe how traders could actually define the parameters for such a signal other than saying that one can initiate a position if a TD Sell Setup holds TDST resistance on a closing basis. As earlier with the TD Buy Setups, however, I have my own set of very clear rules for trading TD Sell Setups objectively.

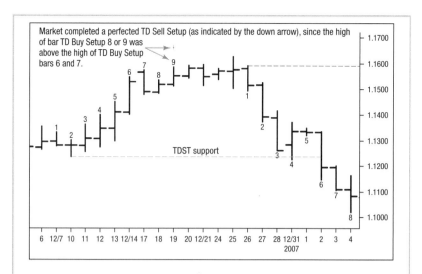

FIGURE 1.12 **Perfected TD Sell Setup**

In the chart of USDCHF, the market records a perfected TD Sell Setup bar nine, because the highs of TD Sell Setup bars eight or nine are above the highs of TD Sell Setup bars six and seven.

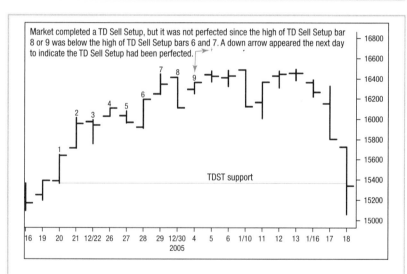

FIGURE 1.13 **Unperfected TD Sell Setup**

In the chart of the Nikkei 225, the market reaches TD Sell Setup bar nine, but the TD Sell Setup is not perfected, because the highs of TD Sell Setup bars eight or nine are not greater than the highs of TD Sell Setup bars six and seven. This pattern shows that there is an increased risk that the market could come back to retest the greater of bars six and seven before the expected consolidation/reversal materializes. The reversal materializes the following day, and the down arrow above the subsequent bar indicates where the TD Sell Setup is eventually perfected.

15

First, although many people mistakenly believe that one should initiate a short position following every completed TD Sell Setup, I advise against that except under the following conditions.

■ Perl's Rules on When to Initiate a Short Position Following a Completed TD Sell Setup

1. When the TD Sell Setup has been perfected, that is, when the high of TD Sell Setup bar eight or nine is greater than the highs of TD Sell Setup bars six and seven,

2. When none of the bars within the TD Sell Setup has closed above TDST resistance, and

3. When the close of TD Buy Setup bar nine is in close proximity to TDST resistance.

As with the TD Buy Setup, I have my own preference, that is, for the close of TD Sell Setup bar nine to be higher than the close of TD Sell Setup bar eight, but this is optional (**Figure 1.14**).

Next, assuming the above conditions are met, and the signal is triggered on TD Sell Setup bar nine, the TD risk level for such a trade must be calculated.

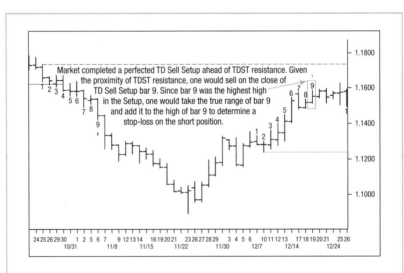

FIGURE 1.14   **Trading a Perfected TD Sell Setup**

In the chart of USDCHF, the market records a perfected TD Sell Setup ahead of TDST resistance.

▨ Risk Management: Calculating the TD Risk Level for a TD Sell Setup

1. Identify the TD Sell Setup bar with the highest true high, and
2. Add the true range of that bar to its true high.

(If, for example, TD Sell Setup bar eight has the highest true high, add the true range of that bar to its true high, to derive the TD Sell risk level.)

The expectation would be for a return toward the lower-range extreme, as defined by TDST support—in other words, the true low of the most recently completed TD Sell Setup.

Typically, I would take the trade only if the difference between the entry price—the close of TD Sell Setup bar nine—and TDST support is more than 1.5 times the difference between the TD risk level and the close of TD Sell Setup bar nine.

TD Setup vs. TD Sequential Countdown

Once TD Setup is complete, TD Countdown can begin, from the close of bar nine of TD Setup (inclusive), onward. The distinction between the two strategies is this:

• **TD Setup** compares the current close with the corresponding close four bars earlier,

Whereas

• **TD Countdown** compares the current close with the low two bars earlier for a potential buy, and compares the current close with the high two bars earlier for a prospective sell. This price relationship is an important distinction from TD Setup, because the market must be trending for TD Countdown to objectively identify the likely exhaustion point for a trend reversal.

One can start looking for the first bar of a TD Buy Countdown when a TD Buy Setup is in place.

▨ To Initiate TD Buy Countdown

After

TD Buy Setup is in place, look for the initiation of a TD Buy Countdown.

If

Bar nine of a TD Buy Setup also has a close less than, or equal to, the low two bars earlier,

Then,

Bar nine of a TD Buy Setup becomes bar one of a TD Buy Countdown.

If

That condition is not met,

Then

TD Buy Countdown bar one is postponed until it does, and the TD Buy Countdown continues until there are a total of thirteen closes, each one less than, or equal to, the low two bars earlier.

Unlike TD Buy Setup, TD Buy Countdown doesn't have to be an uninterrupted sequence of qualifying price bars; the TD Buy Countdown process simply stops when markets are trading sideways, and resumes when prices start trending lower again.

For a TD Buy Countdown to be completed (**Figures 1.15** and **1.16**) and to help identify a low-risk buying opportunity, bar thirteen must meet certain requirements.

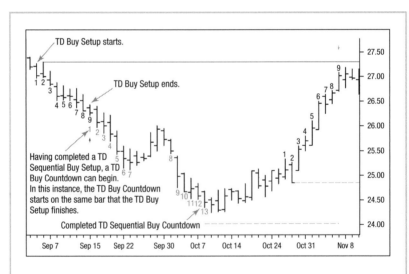

FIGURE 1.15   **Completed TD Sequential Buy Countdown**

In the chart of Microsoft, subsequent to the completed TD Buy Setup, the market records a series of thirteen closes, each one less than, or equal to, the low two price bars earlier, thereby completing a TD Sequential Buy Countdown.

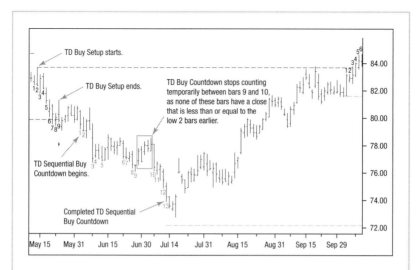

FIGURE 1.16   **Completed TD Sequential Buy Countdown**

In the chart of IBM, the market completes a TD Buy Setup, but price doesn't satisfy the conditions to begin a TD Buy Countdown until seven days later. Consequently, the TD Buy Countdown phase is deferred until that condition (that is, a close less than, or equal to, the low two price bars earlier) is fulfilled.

Note: When there is an interruption in the sequence of closes that are less than, or equal to, the lows two price bars earlier, the TD Buy Countdown phase stops until the conditions are met again, at which point counting can resume—as is the case in this instance, between TD Buy Countdown bars 9 and 10.

▥ To Complete a TD Buy Countdown

1. The low of TD Buy Countdown bar thirteen must be less than, or equal to, the close of TD Buy Countdown bar eight, and

2. The close of TD Buy Countdown bar thirteen must be less than, or equal to, the low two bars earlier.

When the market fails to meet these conditions, the thirteen is deferred, and a plus sign (+) appears where the number thirteen would otherwise have been.

It can be extremely frustrating to see the market recover following a "deferred thirteen," while the trader is still waiting for a buy signal.

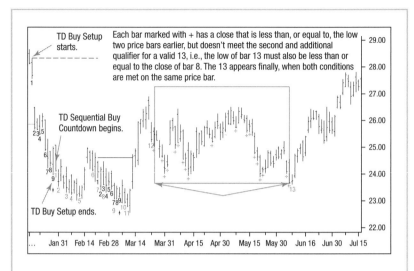

FIGURE 1.17   **Deferred TD Sequential Buy Countdown**

In the chart of Microsoft, subsequent to the completed TD Buy Setup, the market begins a series of closes, each one less than, or equal to, the low two price bars earlier. After bar twelve, however, a plus sign appears, indicating that TD Buy Countdown bar thirteen has been deferred. When a plus sign appears beneath a TD Buy Countdown bar, it means that although the close is less than, or equal to, the low two price bars earlier, the market fails to satisfy the other condition that is required to produce a thirteen (that the low of TD Buy Countdown bar thirteen be less than, or equal to, the close of TD Buy Countdown bar eight). Only when the same price bar satisfies both conditions does the TD Buy Countdown bar thirteen appear.

However, as long as a plus sign is present in lieu of a bar labeled thirteen, there is a heightened risk that the market will revisit the close of a TD Buy Countdown bar eight before a reversal materializes (**Figure 1.17**).

A more conservative approach would also require the low of TD Buy Countdown bar eight to be less than, or equal to, the close of TD Buy Countdown bar five, but DeMark considers this an elective option rather than a prerequisite.

Patience and discipline should always rule the day. Never preempt a signal. As my former colleague David Toth used to say, "Better to be out of a trade, wishing you were in it, than to be in a trade, wishing you were out of it."

TD Buy Countdown Cancellation

Although a developing TD Buy Countdown doesn't reset itself if there is an interruption in the sequence of closes each one of which is less than, or equal to, the low two bars earlier, there are a number of built-in conditions, or filters, to help the trader recognize when the dynamics of the market are changing. These filters erase the as-yet-incomplete TD Buy Countdown.

▨ Filters That Cancel a Developing TD Buy Countdown

Either of the following conditions erases an incomplete TD Buy Countdown:

1. If the price action rallies and generates a TD Sell Setup, or
2. If the market trades higher and posts a true low above the true high of the prior TD Buy Setup—that is, TDST resistance.

DeMark is currently investigating a subtle change here, whereby the four price bars prior to the start of the TD Buy Setup would also be included, to determine the reference level for the TD Setup extreme; that is, the market would need a true low above the true high of the prior TD Buy Setup, including the four price bars prior to bar one of the TD Buy Setup.

TD Buy Countdown Cancellation and Recycle Qualifiers

Compare the true range of the previous TD Buy Setup, that is, the difference between the highest true high and the lowest true low, with the true range of the most recently completed TD Buy Setup, and then apply the TD Buy Countdown Cancellation qualifiers I and II.

▨ TD Buy Countdown Cancellation Qualifier I

If

The size of the true range of the most recently completed TD Buy Setup is equal to, or greater than, the size of the previous TD Buy Setup, but less than 1.618 times its size,

Then

A TD Setup Recycle will occur; that is, whichever TD Buy Setup has the larger true range will become the active TD Buy Setup.

When comparing the respective ranges, keep in mind that a TD Buy Setup can extend beyond TD Setup bar nine, if there is no subsequent TD Price Flip to extinguish it.

■ **TD Buy Countdown Cancellation Qualifier II (a TD Buy Setup Within a TD Buy Setup)**

If

The market has completed a TD Buy Setup that has a closing range within the true range of the prior TD Buy Setup, without recording a TD Sell Setup between the two,

And if

The current TD Buy Setup has a price extreme within the true range of the prior TD Buy Setup,

Then

The prior TD Buy Setup is the active TD Setup, and the TD Buy Countdown relating to it remains intact.

When comparing ranges, keep in mind that, as with TD Cancellation Qualifier I, a TD Buy Setup can extend beyond TD Setup bar nine if there is no TD Price Flip to extinguish it.

TD Buy Countdown
Recycle Qualifier

The letter *R* (for recycle) will appear on a chart (**Figure 1.18**) where TD Buy Countdown bar thirteen would otherwise have been if the following condition is met.

■ **An *R* Will Appear**

When a TD Buy Setup that began *before, on,* or *after* the completion of a developing TD Buy Countdown, but *prior* to a bullish TD Price Flip, extends to eighteen bars— that is, eighteen closes, with each one less than the close four price bars earlier.

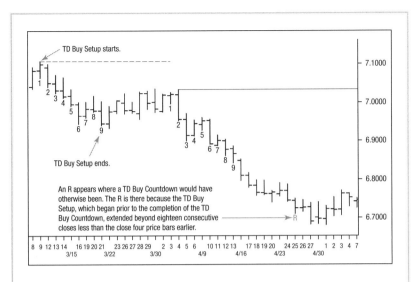

FIGURE 1.18   **Extension of TD Buy Setup from Nine to Eighteen Recycles a Developing TD Buy Countdown**

In the chart of USDSEK, rather than stopping at nine consecutive closes each less than the close four price bars earlier, the second TD Buy Setup, which begins prior to the completion of the TD Buy Countdown, extends to eighteen closes each one less than the close four price bars earlier. This suggests selling pressure is gaining momentum and therefore recycles the TD Buy Countdown. The letter *R* now appears where the TD Sequential Buy Countdown bar thirteen would otherwise have been.

Such an occurrence is meaningful, because it is an acknowledgment that momentum is very strong, and the underlying bear trend has intensified.

There is a misconception that the TD Setup process stops once the count reaches nine. In actual fact, the TD Buy Setup process can continue indefinitely, as long as the uninterrupted series of closes, each one of which is less than the close four price bars earlier, persists.

While charting systems default to display TD Buy Setups only up to bar nine, the Setup continues until a downside TD Price Flip occurs.

Note: The extent of a TD Setup beyond nine can be seen by checking the TD Setup shading box in the TD Sequential properties section and highlighting the area covered by consecutive closes each one less than the close four price bars earlier.

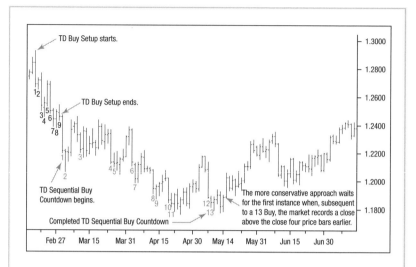

FIGURE 1.19   **Aggressive Approach to Entering a Long Position After a Completed TD Buy Countdown**

In the chart of EURUSD, the market completes a TD Buy Countdown, and a long position is established on the close of TD Buy Countdown bar thirteen (aggressive approach). The more conservative approach is to wait for a confirmed bullish TD Price Flip subsequent to the thirteen (that is, a close greater than the close four price bars earlier), to eliminate the risk of prices recycling.

Entering a Long Position

Following a completed TD Sequential Buy Countdown thirteen, traders can initiate a long position (**Figure 1.19**) using one of the following options (my personal preference being "aggressive").

▪ Two Ways to Enter a Long Position

Aggressive Approach: Buy on the close of a TD Buy Countdown bar thirteen, or

Conservative Approach: Subsequent to a TD Sequential Buy Countdown thirteen, wait for the first instance when the close is greater than the close four price bars earlier—i.e., a bullish TD Price Flip.

Although the latter approach may provide a less-efficient entry point, it eliminates the risk that the market will recycle.

Alternative Strategy for Entering a Long Position

As alternatives, DeMark suggests you can enter a long position using TD Camouflage, TD Clop, TD Clopwin, TD Open, or TD Trap, all of which are described below. You can use all these indicators in isolation, but they are more powerful when used in conjunction with TD Sequential or TD Combo signal.

■ Requirements for a TD Camouflage Buy

1. The close of the current price bar must be below the close of the previous price bar,
2. The close of the current price bar must be above the open of the current price bar, and
3. The low of the current price bar must be lower than true low two price bars earlier.

When this pattern is confirmed, you would initiate long positions on the close.

A TD Clop buy signal works on the assumption that upside momentum will continue when the market exceeds the open and close price of the prior price bar.

■ Requirements for a TD Clop Buy Signal

1. The open of the current price bar must be below the close and open of the previous price bar, and
2. The market must subsequently trade above both the open and close of the previous bar.

If these conditions are met, there is a greater chance that upside momentum will continue into the close.

A TD Clopwin buy signal examines the relationship between the open and close of the current price bar and the open and close of the previous price bar.

■ **Requirements for a TD Clopwin Buy Signal**

1. The open and close of the current price bar must be contained within the open and close range of the previous price bar, and

2. The close of the current price bar must be above the close of the prior price bar.

Meeting these conditions increases the probability that upside momentum will be sustained into the next price bar, thereby reinforcing the TD Sequential buy signal.

■ **Requirements for a TD Open Buy Signal**

1. The current price bar's open must be less than the low of the prior price bar, and

2. It must then trade above that low.

■ **Requirements for a TD Trap Buy Signal**

The open of the current price bar

1. Must be within the range of the previous price bar, and

2. Must then break above the high of that range.

TD Buy Termination Count

I prefer to compare the close of TD Buy Countdown bar thirteen with the low two price bars earlier, but a more aggressive version of Termination Count, which DeMark recommends, is to compare the open on TD Buy Countdown bar thirteen with the low two days earlier.

■ **Risk Management: For a TD Buy Countdown**

Following a completed TD Sequential Buy Countdown:

1. Identify the lowest true low throughout the TD Sequential Buy Countdown process, which includes bars one through thirteen, whether or not it is a numbered price bar;

2. Calculate the difference between the true high and true low for that bar; and

3. Subtract that true range from its true low.

Many traders take the value of the true range of the bar with the lowest true low and subtract it from the low of TD Buy Countdown bar thirteen, but this would be correct only if TD Buy Countdown bar thirteen happened to have the lowest true low. Accordingly, if TD Buy Countdown bar twelve had the lowest true low, then the correct action would be to take the true range of Countdown bar twelve and subtract it from the low of TD Buy Countdown bar twelve (**Figure 1.20**).

By implication, if markets are experiencing high volatility in the lead-up to the signal, then a wide stop-loss is likely, but, if volatility is low leading up to the signal, then a fairly tight stop-loss is likely. What is significant is that you're letting price action, rather than an arbitrary fixed amount, determine the risk level.

Note: Traders can, for example, still opt to risk 1 percent of capital on a trade, but they should reduce position size to accommodate the required TD Sequential risk level. For example, where the risk on a single position might ordinarily be 1 percent of equity, and the required TD Sequential risk level is 2 percent, traders should halve the amount they would otherwise have traded.

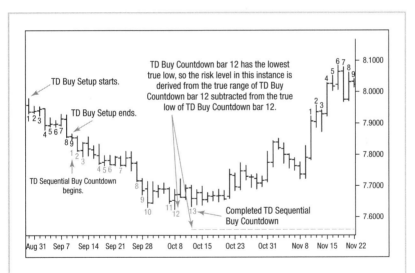

FIGURE 1.20 **Calculating the Risk Level Following a TD Sequential Buy Signal**

In the chart of EURNOK, of all the TD Countdown bars (one to thirteen inclusive as well as those bars that aren't numbered), TD Countdown bar twelve has the lowest true low. To calculate the TD risk level, we therefore take the value of the true range of that bar and subtract it from its true low.

Frequently Asked Questions

What constitutes a valid downside break of a TD Sequential Buy Countdown risk level?

DeMark recommends following these rules to determine a valid downside break (the price bar that violates the TD risk level is bar X):

1. The close of price bar X needs to be below the downside TD risk level,
2. The close of price bar X − 1 must be higher than the close of price bar X − 2,
3. The open of price bar X + 1 must be a down open, and
4. The low of price bar X + 1 must be at least one tick below the open of price bar X + 1.

My own preference is to stop out of a long position as soon as the downside risk level is violated on an intrabar basis. From personal experience, I have found that either the TD Buy Countdown risk level holds, or the market accelerates through it. Since there are fewer instances in which the market violates the TD Buy risk level and then reverses, I'd rather know my up-front risk than incur an unknown, potentially substantial loss while I wait for the four-step process above to be satisfied.

How much time should be allowed for the market to respond to a TD Sequential buy signal?

Ideally, the market should have a meaningful response within twelve price bars. A close above the close four price bars earlier eliminates the risk of a TD Recycle, and so that is an important reinforcing factor, but it is preferable for the market to trade above the TD Reference Close (that is, the highest close four price bars before the trend low) up until the point when the buy signal was generated—within twelve price bars of the TD Countdown thirteen buy.

What are the requirements for a TD Sequential 9-13-9 Buy Count?

Following the TD Buy Countdown bar thirteen, the market temporarily trades higher—producing a bullish TD Price Flip—but subsequently trades lower again and goes on to record a TD Buy Setup.

A TD Sequential 9-13-9 Buy Count provides a fresh opportunity to fade the underlying downtrend and initiate a long position, but to validate the signal, the following conditions must occur.

■ Requirements for Validation of a TD Sequential 9-13-9 Buy Count

1. The TD Buy Setup must not begin before or on the same price bar as the completed TD Buy Countdown,

2. The ensuing bullish TD Buy Setup must be preceded by a TD Price Flip, and

3. No completed TD Sell Setup should occur prior to the appearance of the TD Buy Setup.

Once these conditions are satisfied, a fresh long position can be established on the close of the completed TD Sequential 9-13-9 (**Figures 1.21**, **1.22**, and **1.23**). Although DeMark doesn't outline how to

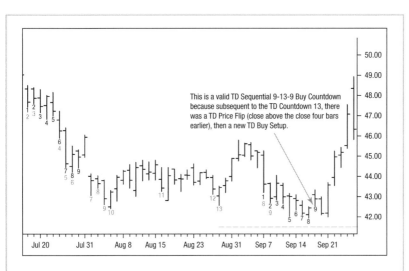

This is a valid TD Sequential 9-13-9 Buy Countdown because subsequent to the TD Countdown 13, there was a TD Price Flip (close above the close four bars earlier), then a new TD Buy Setup.

FIGURE 1.21 **Qualified TD Sequential 9-13-9 Buy Signal**

In the chart of BMW, the market records a TD Sequential Buy Countdown. Although the market rallies initially after generating a bullish TD Price Flip, (that is, a close higher than the close four price bars earlier), the market fails to sustain those gains and, without first having produced a TD Sell Setup, it sells off again to complete a fresh TD Buy Setup, which generates a TD Sequential 9-13-9 buy signal. The signal is particularly compelling because the risk level on the prior TD Sequential Buy Countdown is still intact.

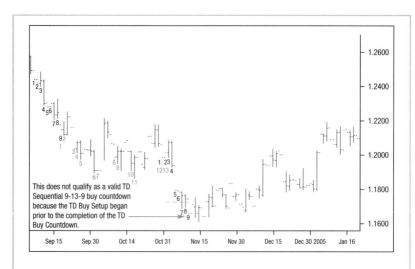

This does not qualify as a valid TD
Sequential 9-13-9 buy countdown
because the TD Buy Setup began
prior to the completion of the TD
Buy Countdown.

FIGURE 1.22 Disqualified TD Sequential 9-13-9 Buy Signal

In the chart of EURUSD, the market completes a TD Buy Setup subsequent to a TD Buy Countdown. Note, however, that because the TD Buy Setup begins prior to the completion of the TD Buy Countdown, this does not qualify as a TD Sequential 9-13-9 buy signal. There is, consequently, no Bullish TD Price Flip separating the TD Buy Setup from the TD Buy Countdown.

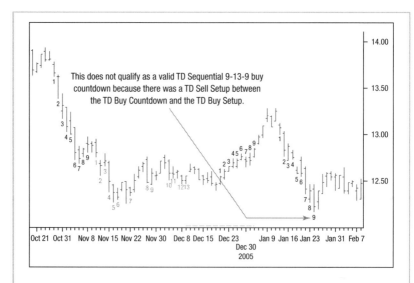

This does not qualify as a valid TD Sequential 9-13-9 buy
countdown because there was a TD Sell Setup between
the TD Buy Countdown and the TD Buy Setup.

FIGURE 1.23 Disqualified TD Sequential 9-13-9 Buy Signal

In the chart of Telefonica, the market completes a TD Buy Countdown. There's a TD Sell Setup, however, between that and the subsequent TD Buy Setup, which means that this does not qualify as a valid TD Sequential 9-13-9 buy signal.

30

determine a risk level for this sort of trade, I have developed my own method.

Risk Management: For TD Sequential 9-13-9

Subtract the true range of the price bar with the lowest true low in the TD Buy Countdown and ensuing TD Buy Setup from the true low of that bar.

TD Sell Countdown

As soon as a TD Sell Setup is in place, we can start looking for the first bar of a TD Sell Countdown; bar nine of a TD Sell Setup can also be bar one of a TD Sell Countdown if it satisfies the following conditions.

Requirement for a TD Sell Countdown

With bar nine of the TD Sell Setup in place, there must be a close greater than, or equal to, the high two bars earlier.

Bar one of the TD Sell Countdown is postponed until the requirement is satisfied. Unlike TD Sell Setup, the TD Sell Countdown doesn't have to be an uninterrupted sequence of qualifying price bars.

The TD Sell Countdown process pauses when markets are trading sideways, resumes when prices start trending higher again, and continues until there is a total of thirteen closes, each one greater than, or equal to, the high two bars earlier (**Figures 1.24** and **1.25**).

To Complete a TD Sell Countdown

1. The high of TD Sell Countdown bar thirteen must be greater than, or equal to, the close of TD Sell Countdown bar eight, and

2. The close of TD Sell Countdown bar thirteen must be greater than, or equal to, the high two bars earlier.

When the market fails to meet these conditions, TD Sell Countdown bar thirteen is deferred, and a plus sign appears where

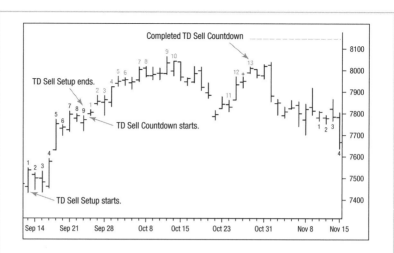

FIGURE 1.24 **Completed TD Sequential Sell Countdown**

In the chart of the German DAX Index, subsequent to the completed TD Sell Setup, the market goes on to record a series of thirteen closes, each one greater than, or equal to, the high two price bars earlier, thereby completing a TD Sequential Sell Countdown.

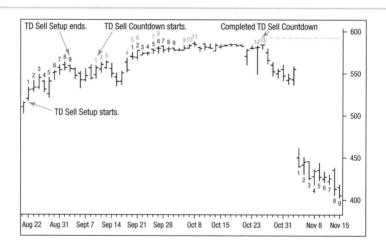

FIGURE 1.25 **Completed TD Sequential Sell Countdown**

In the chart of J Sainsbury PLC, the market completes a TD Sell Setup, but the price doesn't satisfy the conditions to begin a TD Sell Countdown until five bars later. Consequently, the TD Sell Countdown phase is deferred until that condition—a close greater than or equal to the high two price bars earlier—is fulfilled. Note that when there is an interruption in the TD Sell Countdown sequence of closes greater than, or equal to, the high two price bars earlier, the TD Sell Countdown phase stops until the conditions are met again. At that point counting can resume; in this case the interruption occurs between TD Sell Countdown bars eleven and twelve.

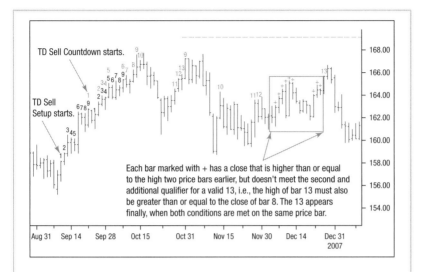

TD Sell Countdown starts.

TD Sell Setup starts.

Each bar marked with + has a close that is higher than or equal to the high two price bars earlier, but doesn't meet the second and additional qualifier for a valid 13, i.e., the high of bar 13 must also be greater than or equal to the close of bar 8. The 13 appears finally, when both conditions are met on the same price bar.

| Aug 31 | Sep 14 | Sep 28 | Oct 15 | Oct 31 | Nov 15 | Nov 30 | Dec 14 | Dec 31 2007 |

FIGURE 1.26   **Deferred TD Sequential Sell Countdown**

In the chart of EURJPY, subsequent to the completed TD Sell Setup, the market begins a series of closes, each one greater than, or equal to, the high two price bars earlier. However, after TD Sell Countdown bar twelve, a plus sign appears, indicating TD Sell Countdown bar thirteen has been deferred. In the instances of a bar marked with a plus sign, the close is greater than, or equal to, the high two price bars earlier, but the market has failed to satisfy the additional condition necessary to produce a bar thirteen: The high of TD Sell Countdown bar thirteen must also be greater than, or equal to, the close of TD Buy Countdown bar eight. Only when one price bar satisfies both conditions does the TD Sell Countdown bar thirteen appear.

TD Sell Countdown bar thirteen would have otherwise been (**Figure 1.26**).

It can be extremely frustrating to see the market decline after a "deferred thirteen," when a sell signal has still not appeared. However, as long as a plus sign is present in lieu of a bar labeled thirteen, there is a heightened risk the market will revisit the close of a TD Sell Countdown bar eight before a reversal materializes.

A more conservative approach would also require the high of TD Sell Countdown bar eight to be greater than, or equal to, the close of TD Sell Countdown bar five, but DeMark considers this an elective option rather than a prerequisite.

TD Sell Countdown Cancellation

Although a developing TD Sell Countdown doesn't reset itself if there is an interruption in the sequence of closes greater than, or equal to, the high two bars earlier, built-in filters recognize when the dynamics of the market are changing. These filters cancel the as-yet-incomplete TD Sell Countdown.

■ Filters That Will Cancel a Developing TD Sell Countdown

Either of the following conditions erases an incomplete TD Sell Countdown:

If

Price action leads to a selloff, and a TD Buy Setup is generated,

Or

The market trades lower, and posts a true high, below the true low of the prior TD Sell Setup (that is, TDST support).

DeMark is currently investigating a subtle change to this indicator, whereby the four price bars prior to the start of the TD Sell Setup are also included, to determine the reference level for the TD Sell Setup extreme; that is, the market would need a true high below the true low of the prior TD Sell Setup, including the four price bars prior to bar one of the TD Sell Setup.

TD Sell Countdown Cancellation
and Recycle Qualifiers

Compare the true range of the previous TD Sell Setup, that is, the difference between the highest true high and the lowest true low, with the true range of the most recently completed TD Sell Setup, and then apply the TD Sell Countdown Cancellation qualifiers I and II.

■ TD Sell Countdown Cancellation Condition I

If

The size of the true range of the most recently completed TD Sell Setup is equal to, or greater than, the size of the previous TD Sell Setup, but less than 1.618 times as big,

Then

A TD Countdown Cancellation will occur. Whichever TD Sell Setup has the larger true range will become the active TD Sell Setup.

TD Sell Countdown Cancellation Condition II (a TD Sell Setup Within a TD Sell Setup)

If

The market completes a TD Sell Setup with a closing range within the true range of the prior TD Sell Setup, without recording a TD Buy Setup between the two, and the current TD Sell Setup has an extreme close, to close range within the true range of the prior TD Sell Setup,

Then

The prior TD Sell Setup is the active TD Setup, and the TD Sell Countdown related to it remains intact.

When comparing the respective ranges, as with TD Cancellation qualifier condition I, take into consideration that TD Sell Setup can extend beyond nine if there is no TD Price Flip to extinguish it.

TD Sell Countdown Recycle Qualifier

Following a complete TD Sequential Sell Countdown thirteen, traders can initiate a short position using either the aggressive or conservative approach, my personal preference being the aggressive.

If

A TD Sell Setup extends to eighteen bars (that is, eighteen closes each one greater than the close four price bars earlier prior to the occurrence of a TD Price Flip),

Then

The prior TD Sell Countdown is negated and the letter *R* will appear on the chart where TD Sell Countdown bar thirteen would have otherwise been.

Note: The appearance of the R *is meaningful because it is an acknowledgement that momentum is very strong and the underlying bull trend has intensified* (**Figure 1.27**).

Entering a Short Position Following a Completed Thirteen TD Sequential Sell Countdown

Aggressive Approach: Sell on the close of TD Sell Countdown bar thirteen or

Conservative Approach: Subsequent to a TD Countdown thirteen, wait for the first instance in which the close is less than the close four price bars earlier—i.e., a bearish TD Price Flip.

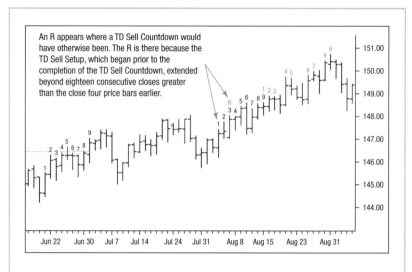

FIGURE 1.27   Extension of TD Sell Setup from Nine to Eighteen Recycles a Developing TD Sell Countdown

In the chart of EURJPY, rather than stopping at nine consecutive closes, each greater than the close four price bars earlier, the TD Sell Setup extends to eighteen closes, each greater than the close four price bars earlier. This suggests buying pressure is gaining momentum, and therefore the TD Sell Countdown is recycled. The letter *R* now appears where the TD Sequential Sell Countdown thirteen would have been.

While the conservative approach eliminates the risk of the market's recycling, it provides a less efficient entry point, and hence my preference for the more aggressive approach (**Figure 1.28**).

Alternative Strategy for Entering a Short Position

DeMark suggests you can enter a short position using TD Camouflage, TD Clop, TD Clopwin, TD Open, or TD Trap, each of which can be used alone but is more powerful used in conjunction with TD Sequential or TD Combo Signals.

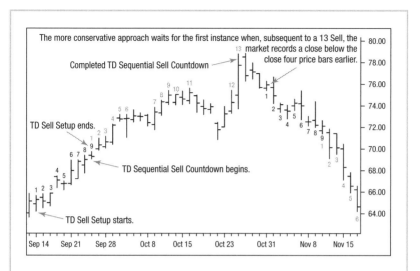

The more conservative approach waits for the first instance when, subsequent to a 13 Sell, the market records a close below the close four price bars earlier.

Completed TD Sequential Sell Countdown

TD Sell Setup ends.

TD Sequential Sell Countdown begins.

TD Sell Setup starts.

FIGURE 1.28 **Aggressive Approach for Entering a Short Position After a Completed TD Sell Countdown**

In the chart of Daimler, the market completes a TD Sell Countdown, and a short position is established on the close of TD Sell Countdown bar thirteen.

Conservative approach for entering a short position after a completed TD Sell Countdown. Rather than establishing a short position on the close of TD Sell Countdown bar thirteen, the more conservative approach is to wait for a confirmed bearish TD Price Flip—subsequent to the thirteen—that is, a close less than the close four price bars earlier, to eliminate the risk that prices will recycle.

TD Camouflage Sell Signal Requirements

1. The close of the current price bar must be above the close of the previous price bar,

2. The close of the current price bar must be below the open of the current price bar open, and

3. The high of the current price bar high must be above the true high two price bars earlier.

Short positions would be initiated on the close when this pattern has been confirmed.

■ TD Clop Sell Signal Requirements

1. Downside momentum must continue when the market exceeds the open and close price of the prior price bar,

2. The open of the current price bar must be above the close of the previous price bar and open, and

3. The market must subsequently trade below both the open and close of the previous price bar.

Meeting these conditions increases the probability that downward momentum will continue into the close.

■ TD Clopwin Sell Signal Requirements

1. The open and close of the current price bar must be contained within the open and close range of the previous price bar, and

2. The close of the current price bar must be below the close of the prior price bar.

Meeting these conditions increases the probability that downward momentum will be sustained into the next price bar, thereby reinforcing the TD Sequential sell signal.

■ TD Open Sell Signal Requirements

1. The open of the current price bar must be above the high of the prior price bar, and

2. It must then trade below that high.

■ TD Trap Sell Signal Requirements

1. The current price bar's open must be within the previous price bar's range, and

2. It must then break below the low of that range.

TD Sell Termination Count

I prefer to compare the close of TD Sell Countdown bar thirteen with the high two price bars earlier. DeMark recommends the more aggressive open setting, which compares the open of TD Countdown bar thirteen with the high two price bars earlier.

▓ Risk Management: For a TD Sell Countdown

Following a completed TD Sequential Sell Countdown,

1. Identify the highest true high throughout the TD Sequential Sell Countdown process, which includes bars one through thirteen, whether or not it is a numbered price bar,

2. Calculate the difference between the true high and true low (the range) for that bar, and

3. Add that true range to its true high.

Do not take the value of the true range of the bar with the highest true high and add it to the high of TD Sell Countdown bar thirteen—unless TD Sell Countdown bar thirteen happens to have the highest true high, such as, for example, if TD Sell Countdown bar twelve has the highest true high. If this occurs, you would take the true range of TD Sell Countdown bar twelve and add it to the high of TD Sell Countdown bar twelve.

By implication, if markets are experiencing high volatility in the lead-up to the signal, then a wide stop-loss is likely, but, if volatility is low leading up to the signal, then a fairly tight stop-loss is likely. The key factor is that you're letting price action—rather than an arbitrary fixed amount—determine the risk level (**Figure 1.29**). You can still opt to risk the same percentage of capital, but you should reduce position size relative to the required TD Sequential risk level. For example, if you would ordinarily risk 1 percent of equity on a single position, and the TD Sequential risk level is 2 percent, then halve the amount you would otherwise have traded.

Frequently Asked Questions

What constitutes a valid break of a TD Sequential Sell Countdown risk level?

To determine a valid upside break, DeMark recommends the following (the price bar that violates the TD Sell risk level to the upside is bar X):

1. That the close of price bar X be above the TD Sell risk level,
2. That the close of price bar $X - 1$ be lower than the close of price bar $X - 2$,

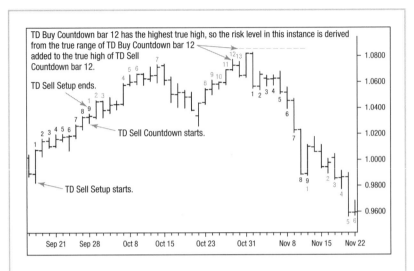

FIGURE 1.29 **Calculation of the Risk Level Following a TD Sequential Sell Signal**

In the chart of AUDCHF, bar twelve of TD Countdown bars one through thirteen (which include all bars, numbered or not) has the highest true high. To calculate the TD risk level, add the value of the true range of that bar to the value of its true high.

3. That the open of price bar X + 1 be an up open, and
4. That the high of price bar X + 1 be at least one tick above its open.

My preference is to stop out of a short position as soon as the upside risk level is violated on an intrabar basis, since, usually, either the TD Sell risk level holds or the market accelerates through it. Only rarely does the market violate the TD Sell risk level and then reverse. I'd prefer knowing my up-front risk than incurring an unknown and potentially substantial loss waiting for the four-step process above to be satisfied.

How much time should be allowed for the market to respond to a TD Sequential sell signal?
Ideally the market should have a meaningful response within twelve price bars. Although a close less than the close four price

bars earlier eliminates the risk of a TD Recycle, and is therefore an important reinforcing factor, it is preferable that the market trade below the TD Reference Close, that is, the lowest close four price bars before the trend high, up until the point when the sell signal was generated and within twelve price bars of the TD Countdown thirteen sell.

What are the requirements for TD Sequential 9-13-9 Sell Count?

If, following a TD Sell Countdown thirteen, the market temporarily trades lower and produces a TD Price Flip and subsequently goes on to record a TD Sell Setup, then what is known as a TD Sequential 9-13-9 Sell Count occurs, which provides a fresh opportunity to fade the underlying uptrend and initiate a short position.

Requirements for Validating a TD Sequential 9-13-9 Sell Count

1. The TD Sell Setup must not begin before or on the same price bar as the completed TD Sell Countdown,

2. The ensuing TD Sell Setup must be preceded by a bearish TD Price Flip, and

3. There must be no completed TD Buy Setup prior to the appearance of the TD Sell Setup.

To allow the establishment of a fresh short position on the close of the completed TD Sequential 9-13-9, the TD Sequential 9-13-9 Sell Count must be validated (**Figures 1.30**, **1.31**, and **1.32**).

Risk Management: For a TD Sequential 9-13-9 Sell Count

Although DeMark doesn't outline how to determine a risk level for this sort of trade, my preference is to:

Add the true range of the price bar with the highest true high in the TD Sell Countdown and subsequent TD Sell Setup to the true high of that bar, and to use that as my risk level.

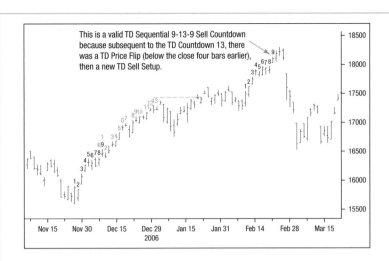

FIGURE 1.30 **Qualified TD Sequential 9-13-9 Sell Signal**

In the chart of the Nikkei 225, the market records a TD Sequential Sell Countdown. Although exhibiting an initial decline after generating a Bearish TD Price Flip—that is, a close less than the close four price bars earlier—the market fails to sustain those losses and, without having first produced a TD Buy Setup, rallies again, to complete a fresh TD Sell Setup, and thereby generate a TD Sequential 9-13-9 Sell Signal.

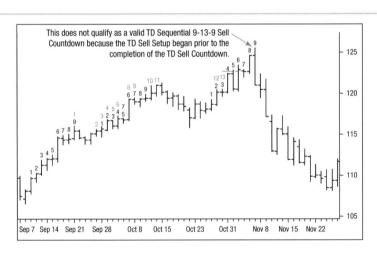

FIGURE 1.31 **Disqualified TD Sequential 9-13-9 Sell Signal**

In the chart of CADJPY, although the market completes a TD Sell Setup subsequent to the TD Sell Countdown, note that the TD Sell Setup begins prior to the completion of the TD Sell Countdown. Because of this and because the market consequently exhibits no Bearish TD Price Flip separating the TD Sell Setup from the TD Sell Countdown, the signal is not, therefore, a TD Sequential 9-13-9.

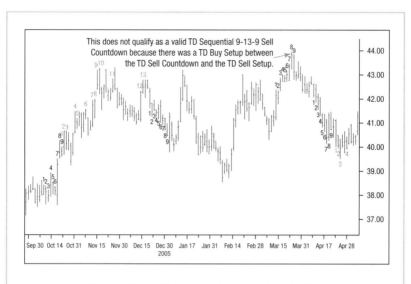

FIGURE 1.32 **Disqualified TD Sequential 9-13-9 Sell Signal**

In the chart of The Home Depot U.S.A., although the market completes a TD Sell Countdown, there's a TD Buy Setup between that and the subsequent TD Sell Setup, which is an event that renders the TD Sequential 9-13-9 Sell signal invalid.

Combining Time Frames for Additional Confidence

Applying the approach outlined above to multiple time frames can increase the signal's probability of success (**Figures 1.33**, **1.34**, **1.35**). On March 5, 2007, for example, at a Bloomberg "Thursday Night Technicals" session (type <TNTS> <GO> on your Bloomberg terminal for further details), I highlighted my reasons for being bearish on the USD Index. The USD Index (DXY) already had an active monthly TD Sell Setup at 91.57 from November 2005 (Figure 1.33).

At about the same time, in November 2005, the market also completed a weekly TD Sell Setup, at 91.91 (Figure 1.34). The bear trend was reinforced when DXY violated weekly TDST support at

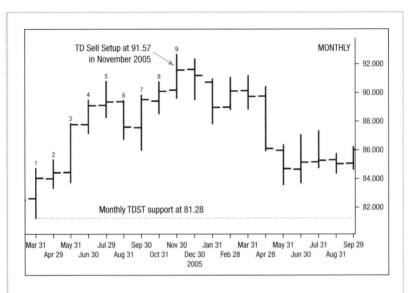

FIGURE 1.33   USD Index (DXY, Basis Cash), Monthly Chart:
Using Multiple Time Frames to Identify the Long-Term
Trend

The confluence of negative DXY signals is reinforced in February 2007, when a
TD Sequential Sell signal occurs at 85.12 on the daily chart. Interestingly, having
violated TDST support in late November 2006, the ensuing sell signal materializes ahead of daily TDST resistance, indicating the market has insufficient upward
momentum for a successful break out of the range to the upside. (See also
Figures 1.34 and 1.35.)

87.75 in April 2006. Finally, on February 12, 2007, having failed
to overcome daily TDST resistance at 85.48, the DXY generated
a daily TD Sequential Sell signal at 85.12 (Figure 1.35). Adding
credence to the bearish view, the market subsequently experienced
a daily close below daily TDST support at 82.38, and posted a
monthly close beneath monthly TDST support at 81.28.

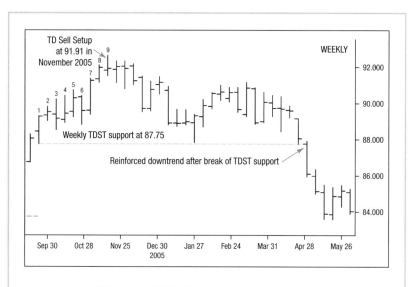

FIGURE 1.34 **USD Index (DXY, Basis Cash) Weekly Chart** (See also
Figures 1.33 and 1.35.)

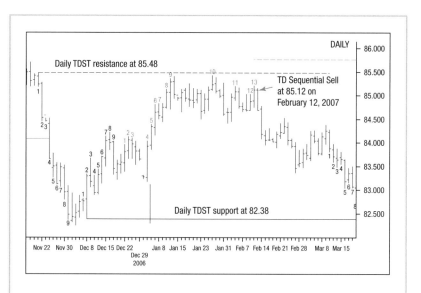

FIGURE 1.35 **USD Index (DXY, Basis Cash) Daily Chart** (See also
Figures 1.33 and 1.34.)

Frequently Asked Questions about TD Sequential

If more people start using TD Sequential, will its usefulness diminish over time?

Consider for a moment that the indicator is countertrend by definition; therefore, it is also counterintuitive for most people who are typically trend followers. Although it's true that a lot of people are now familiar with TD Sequential and look at it on a regular basis, relatively few traders are actually willing to commit capital to it or initiate trades based on it.

If you go long into an uptrend and get stopped out, it's easy to rationalize the position. It looked as if it were going up, and so you bought it, because "the trend is your friend," and other people probably got stopped out too. On the other hand, if you go short into an uptrend and get stopped out, it's harder to justify your actions, particularly since it becomes blatantly apparent retrospectively that the market was entrenched in a directional up move.

There will be times when the indicator doesn't work for prolonged periods, but it is important, nevertheless, not to give up on it, and to remain both disciplined and objective. In the third quarter of 2004, I had had a good run with TD Sequential for a while, but then, in the fourth quarter, I had a series of losing trades. It was a time when many people became despondent and questioned whether the indicator still worked. Well, on January 14, 2005, the indicator gave a buy signal in USDJPY on the New York close.

I should tell you that not only had I been experiencing a particularly bad run of losing recommendations, but it also happened to be a Friday—and not just any Friday, but a Friday before a three-day holiday weekend in the United States. If all that were not enough, the market closed roughly twenty-five pips off a five-year low. From a customer perspective, none of these factors was an ingredient for a high-confidence trade. I think only one of our clients traded the signal that day, and even that client was only closing out a short position, not committing fresh capital to the long side.

I often highlight this example when discussing the indicators—not to say, with hindsight, how wonderful they were—but to illustrate how tough it is to stick with them after a bad run. When you've had a prolonged losing streak, when everyone around you is calling the market lower and questioning the validity of the approach, and when more conventional technical analysis suggests the established trend is firmly intact, you cannot underestimate how difficult it is to take a leap of faith and trade. Think back to my dieting example in the introduction to this book: Even if you know the rules you're supposed to follow, when emotions are involved, it's still not easy to stick with the plan.

How did DeMark come up with nine and thirteen for TD Setup and TD Countdown? Are they necessarily the optimal numbers to use?

Tom DeMark has never really given me a straight answer to the first question—other than to say that his wife, Nancy, was incredibly patient during the time he was developing the indicators. Since the study was done thirty years ago, it's reasonable to ask whether there have been any subsequent optimization tests.

I'm not inclined to optimize the default settings of nine for TD Setup and thirteen for TD Countdown. The fact that you can apply TD Sequential to any market or time frame, irrespective of the market's underlying volatility, without your having to change any of the default parameters, is testimony to how robust it is. Personally, I prefer indicators that work well across the board, rather than studies that are optimized for a specific market or set of conditions; the latter tend to fail when the behavioral characteristics of the market change.

Since DeMark was fascinated by Fibonacci numbers, he had really wanted to use eight for the TD Setup phase, and was disappointed that although nine works better, it's not a Fibonacci number. As mathematicians, designers, and architects know, the Fibonacci numbers are Nature's numbering system, and they are represented in the leaf arrangement of plants, the bracts of a pinecone, and the scales of a pineapple. DeMark was relieved—and able to sleep a lot better—when someone pointed out to him a few years back that, since TD Setups have a four-bar look-back, the TD Setup phase covers thirteen bars in total!

Should I trade every TD Setup nine and TD Countdown thirteen indiscriminately?

It's certainly tempting, but, since TD Sequential is not an infallible indicator, there are times when the signals are less likely to work. My personal preference is to trade a completed TD Setup only if it has been perfected and fails on a close to exceed the prior TD Setup in the opposite direction.

As for TD Countdowns, I try to avoid countertrend signals that coincide with TD Wave 3 (see Chapter 3, "TD D-Wave," for details), unless the projected price target has already been reached and there is reinforcing evidence of price exhaustion from higher-degree TD Sequential time-frame charts.

Is TD Sequential better suited to some markets than others?
I don't believe so; it seems more of a behavioral distinction; that is, some markets have a greater tendency to range trade, and therefore to generate more TD Setups, while others have a greater propensity to trend. The more directional markets produce more TD Countdowns.

Is TD Sequential better suited to some time frames than others?
No. While the indicator was originally developed with daily price data in mind, you can apply it to any time frame from minutes to years, regardless of underlying volatility of the market, and without your having to change any of the default settings. The breadth of its applicability is testimony to the robustness of TD Sequential. I do believe, however, that one's expectations need to be adjusted relative to time frame. Although high-frequency price data will generate a lot of signals and fairly tight risk levels, the expected return per trade is fairly limited; whereas, if you're looking at a longer-term-data series, you'll get fewer signals and greater potential profit per trade—but commensurately wider risk levels.

Have you backtested the performance of TD Sequential signals?
I have not felt the need to backtest the signals, because I've been using the indicators in real time for the past fourteen years. I would encourage those new to the indicators to do so, to get a better sense of when the signals do and do not work. In backtesting, however, bear in mind that you must objectively filter the signals to get confirmation from other TD indicators and, ideally, time frames, and it's up to you to manage the risk and the take-profit level (since DeMark doesn't explain how to manage the trade once it starts to move in your favor). Remember, TD Sequential is an indicator, not a system.

▨ Risk Management for TD Sequential

There are a number of ways in which you can improve the efficiency of the signal without compromising the signal itself:

1. **The "Maximum Favorable and Adverse Excursions Subsequent to a Signal" Method** (that is, the point at which the market goes most in your favor and the point at which it typically goes most against you without being stopped out). This is the most objective way to manage the risk. If you plot the distribution of these variables over time, you can at least determine optimum take-profit levels, which is a useful exercise because there isn't always a signal in the opposite direction to tell you where to close out a profitable trade.

2. **The "Drawdown Support" Method.** (This is the method of risk management popularized by David Stendahl of Rina Systems, and is another concept worth testing.) Rather than tampering with the signal to try to optimize it (which would compromise the integrity of the system), you can try to plot the distribution of signals historically generated. This idea can be applied to any approach. If you notice, for example, that the market often goes half a percent against you before becoming profitable, you could trade half your normal unit size, and then add the remainder (to take you up to what would have been your full initial allocation) when the market reaches the drawdown support level. This way, you remain true to the entry signal, without trying to optimize it, and you remain true to the risk parameters, but you average your entry price. The net effect, over time, should improve your overall performance.

I've noticed, to my cost, that, when markets are trending, most TD Countdown thirteens get stopped out. Is there anything I can do to reduce this risk and improve the success rate of the signals by not trying to fade trends when momentum behind the move is very strong?

Here, instead of using TD Sequential in isolation, I'd suggest using the indicator on a multiple-time-frame basis, to see if higher-degree time frames are in sync with other indicators, such as TD Combo and TD D-Wave. TD D-Wave, in particular, is helpful, because it puts the broader trend into context, and I've observed, over the years, that countertrend TD Sequential signals occurring in TD D-Wave three are more likely to violate their risk levels than those that, for example, coincide with TD D-Wave five.

How important is context?

Just as it's sound from an ecological perspective to consider the environment you live in, it's sound from a trend perspective to consider the market environment you operate in. For me, although weekly, monthly, quarterly, and annual signals are important (particularly when they line up with daily charts), the signals stemming from the dailies are the most important, particularly if you trade intraday. You will improve your chances of success if, for example, you take only buy signals intraday (completed thirteens or nines that hold TDST support), rather than sell signals, if the daily chart has an active qualified buy signal in place.

Should I trade TD Countdown thirteens using short-dated options rather than the underlying cash or futures instrument I get the signal in?

It depends on the circumstances. Often people think an option is a better way to express a countertrend view, because they believe there's a lower probability that the risk level will be violated before the expected reversal materializes. That may be so, but it's also important to consider the time-decay element and the implied volatility of the option in question. I'm inclined to express a countertrend view only following a completed TD Sequential via an option if implied volatility is very low. Otherwise, when you're wrong, you get hit from a price, time, and volatility-decay perspective, if the trend continues more gradually or if the market merely consolidates.

If we're already on bar twelve of a prospective thirteen, why shouldn't I preempt the signal if I think a reversal is imminent?

Let's say the market is on bar twelve of a prospective TD Buy Countdown thirteen. The only thing that would prevent the appearance of a thirteen would be if there were a market rally—the event you were ultimately waiting for. Since, however, the market would need to close less than, or equal to, the low two price bars earlier to complete the signal, it would not be advisable to preempt the signal because:

- There's a risk of new lows, and
- The true range of the lowest low is used to calculate the risk level (which means that, if you act ahead of time, you could quite easily have the wrong stop-loss).

Sometimes a random TD Countdown number seems to appear from nowhere—is this a bug in the software?

No. What's going on here is that, since charting systems are programmed not to display more than one developing TD Countdown at any given

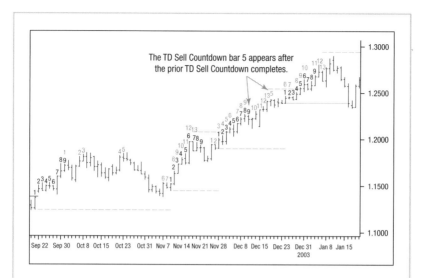

FIGURE 1.36   **A TD Buy Countdown Number "Appearing from Nowhere"**

In the chart of EURUSD, a seemingly random TD Buy Countdown number 5 appears "from nowhere," on December 18, 2003. This isn't a bug; it's part of the TD Buy Countdown resulting from the TD Buy Setup that finishes on December 10, 2003, but the Bloomberg charting system doesn't display that Countdown until the prior Countdown completes.

moment, the default is always to show the TD Countdown closest to completion (**Figure 1.36**). If, for example, there are two TD Countdowns in progress, the second, hidden, TD Countdown will continue counting in the background, but be displayed only when the first TD Countdown finishes (hence making it appear that TD Countdown numbers sometimes appear "from nowhere," midcount).

Sometimes TD Setups and TD Countdowns disappear—is this a bug in the software?

No. When market-data systems update in real time, they treat the current price as the close, which is why a signal that happens to satisfy the requisite criteria on an intrabar basis may appear on a real-time basis prior to the completion of a price bar. The numbers are not fixed until the end of the chosen period, however, and so they will disappear if the necessary conditions are not satisfied at the close of the period selected. Be aware that TD Setups are continually forming, regardless of where we are in the TD Countdown phase.

Can I apply TD Sequential to any price-data series?

Yes, you can, with the proviso that the data needs to be clean, that is, free of any unintentional price gaps or missing data points. In fact, we've had success applying the indicator not only to price, but also to tick charts (which aggregate the number of price updates to allow each bar to represent an equal number of price updates), to constant-volume bars (which aggregate volume data to allow each bar to represent an equal volume), to spreads, to bond yields, to implied volatility, to economic-data series, and even to proprietary data like the UBS FX Risk Index (**Figures 1.37**, **1.38**, **1.39**, and **1.40**).

Can I apply TD Sequential to other technical indicators?

Yes, it's worth experimenting with this idea, but you need to be aware that, by doing so, you're looking at a derivative of price. My preference

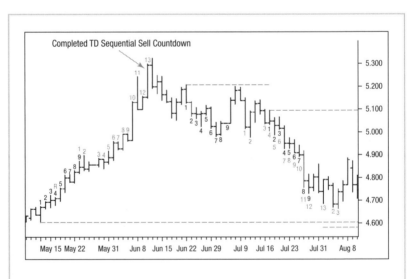

FIGURE 1.37 **Daily Chart of TD Sequential Overlaid on U.S. 10-Year Cash Yields**

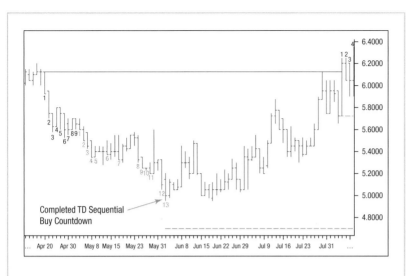

FIGURE 1.38   Daily Chart of TD Sequential Overlaid on EURUSD
3-Month Implied Volatility

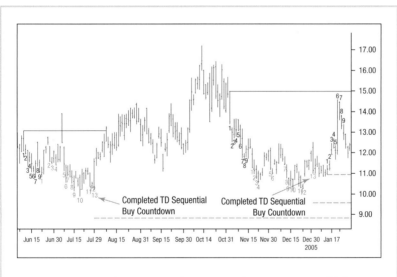

FIGURE 1.39   Daily Chart of TD Sequential Overlaid on the CBOE
S&P 500 VIX (Volatility Index)

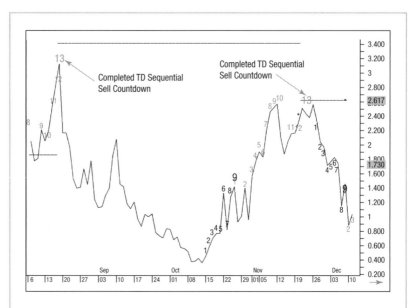

FIGURE 1.40 **Applying TD Sequential to the UBS FX Risk Index**

This daily index chart shows how TD Sequential is successfully applied to the UBS FX Risk Index. The index shows investor appetite for risk. The chart shows that when the index is rising, the market is increasingly risk averse; when the index is falling, the chart reflects a growing appetite for risk. If you apply TD Sequential to the index, as has been done in the past, it's an extremely useful tool to help you identify prospective turns in risk appetite or aversion.

Source: CQG, Inc. © 2008. All rights reserved worldwide. www.cqg.com. Data from UBS AG.

is always to evaluate price action first. Nevertheless, it is possible to overlay TD Sequential on momentum indicators like the RSI, and it also works quite well on point & figure charts. Interestingly, you can overlay TD Sequential even on open interest, and I'd also recommend experimenting with applying Fibonacci retracements to TD Setups (**Figures 1.41, 1.42, 1.43, 1.44**, and **1.45**). Remember, while TD Setups are only displayed up until the close of bar nine, it is worth looking at both the retracements of the one- to nine-range extremes and the completed TD Setup beyond nine (the last only until a TD Price Flip occurs). This range can be highlighted if you check the TD Setup shading box in TD Setup parameters.

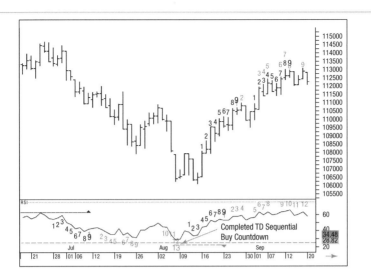

FIGURE 1.41   Using TD Sequential with Overbought or Oversold Oscillators

The daily chart of the S&P 500 (basis cash) shows how you can overlay TD Sequential on overbought or oversold oscillators such as the RSI, to identify prospective turns in momentum. Note how, in this example, if you rely on price alone, you will have no price signal at the low. If you apply TD Sequential to the corresponding RSI, however, you will have evidence that momentum (and therefore price) is susceptible to a reversal higher in August 2004.

Source: CQG, Inc. © 2008. All rights reserved worldwide. www.cqg.com.

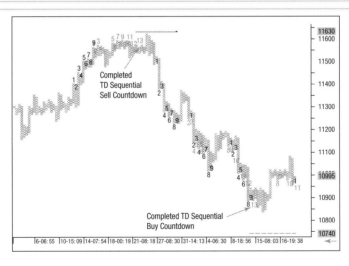

FIGURE 1.42   Using TD Sequential with Point & Figure Charts

The daily chart of USDCHF shows how you can overlay TD Sequential on a point & figure chart to identify prospective turns in price.

Source: CQG, Inc. © 2008. All rights reserved worldwide. www.cqg.com.

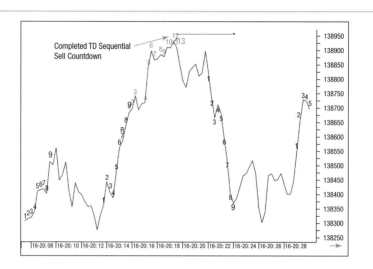

FIGURE 1.43 Using TD Sequential with Tick Charts

The daily chart of the S&P 500 (basis cash) shows how you can overlay TD Sequential on tick charts to identify prospective turns in price. Tick charts aggregate the number of price updates such that each bar represents an equal number of price updates.

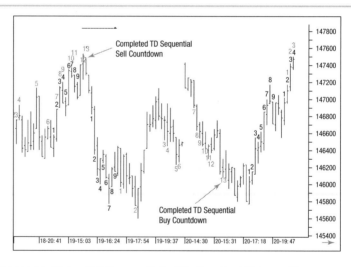

FIGURE 1.44 Using TD Sequential with Constant Volume Bars

The daily chart of the S&P 500 (basis cash) shows how you can overlay TD Sequential on Constant-Volume bars to identify prospective turns in price. Constant volume bars aggregate volume data so that each bar represents the same amount of volume.

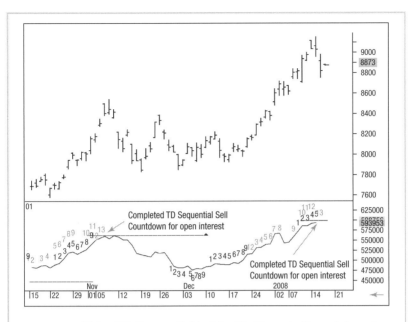

FIGURE 1.45 Using TD Sequential to Identify Turns in Open Interest

The daily chart of COMEX gold shows how you can use TD Sequential even to identify prospective turns in open interest.

Source: CQG, Inc. © 2008. All rights reserved worldwide. www.cqg.com.

TD Sequential: Recommended Settings

Setup | Countdown | Recycle | TDST

Minimum Number of Bars for Setup	9	☒ Show Setup
Number of Bars to Look Back	4	☐ Setup Shading
Setup Price	Close	☐ Setup Perfection Arrows
Show Setup Bars to	Minimum Number of Bars	
Setup Cancel Rule	TrueLow vs TrueHigh	☐ Include Prior Four Bars
☒ Reverse Setup Cancel		

Setup | Countdown | Recycle | TDST

☒ Show Countdown		☐ Countdown Completion Arrows
Number of Bars for Countdown	13	☐ Show Countdown Bars After Minimum
Number of Bars to Look Back	2	☒ Termination Qualifier
Termination Count	Close	☐ 8 vs 5 Qualifier
Countdown Price	Close	
Show Risk Level	Use All Bars in Countdown	

TD Aggressive Sequential

There will inevitably be times when TD Sequential is silent. For those who want to trade more frequently, TD Aggressive Sequential can be a useful adjunct to its more conservative partner. It is very similar to TD Sequential, in the sense that the conditions required to complete the TD Setup phase are the same; it's just the TD Countdown phase that differs.

■ TD Aggressive Sequential

For a prospective sell following a completed TD Sell Setup:

TD Aggressive Sequential compares the high with the high two price bars earlier, during the TD Sell Countdown process.

For a prospective buy following a completed TD Buy Setup:

TD Aggressive Sequential compares the low with the low two price bars earlier during the TD Buy Countdown phase.

By definition, TD Aggressive Sequential always produces buy and sell signals before TD Sequential does. I have found that often TD Aggressive Sequential identifies the trend extreme, while TD Sequential captures the retest of that price extreme. It is generally safer to act when both indicators produce signals at the same time. That said, TD Aggressive Sequential is useful when markets reach price projections, and the relative positioning of the TD studies suggests a reversal is likely, even though TD Sequential is silent.

CHAPTER 2

TD Combo

LIKE ITS COUNTERPART, TD Sequential, TD Combo tries to anticipate price exhaustion within a trend. Because, by definition, it takes a minimum of twenty-two price bars to generate a TD Sequential signal, it is useful to have another tool to identify prospective turning points following an abrupt price movement. Although the criteria necessary to generate a TD Combo buy or sell signal are more stringent than those to complete a TD Sequential Buy or Sell Countdown, TD Combo is better equipped to respond to sharp directional moves, since it requires a minimum of only thirteen price bars from start to finish.

Ideally, a confluence of TD Sequential and TD Combo signals will improve the chance of a successful trade. As with TD Aggressive Sequential, however, there are times when TD Combo speaks and TD Sequential is silent. In such instances, I prefer to have reinforcing evidence of potential price exhaustion from other TD indicators/time frames rather than to rely on the signal in isolation. DeMark suggests that, for intraday charts, TD Combo has a slight edge over TD Sequential.

Note: There are two versions of TD Combo, one more conservative than the other.

TD Combo Buy Setup

The criteria for a TD Buy Setup within TD Combo are identical to those required for a TD Buy Setup within TD Sequential, and for Recycle:

■ Requirements for a TD Combo Buy Setup

First, we need to see a Bearish TD Price Flip, that is, a close above the close four price bars earlier immediately followed by a close beneath the close four price bars earlier.

Then, to complete a TD Buy Setup, starting from and inclusive of the Bearish TD Price Flip bar, we need an uninterrupted series of nine closes, each one lower than the close four price bars earlier.

Differences in Buy Countdown: TD Combo vs. TD Sequential

Once the TD Combo Buy Setup is complete, the differences between TD Combo and TD Sequential become apparent:

- **TD Sequential** waits for the completion of a TD Buy Setup and then begins looking for the conditions necessary to satisfy the requirements for a TD Buy Countdown, but
- **TD Combo** waits for a TD Buy Setup to finish, and then begins the TD Buy Countdown, from bar one of the preceding TD Buy Setup onward.

TD Combo Buy Countdown

Commencing from bar one of the prior qualifying TD Buy Setup, the TD Buy Countdown phase of TD Combo begins retrospectively **(Figure 2.1)**. Unlike TD Sequential, however, which simply states that each close must be less than the corresponding low two price bars earlier, a TD Combo Buy requires four conditions to be satisfied simultaneously. There are two versions, one less strict than the other.

■ Requirements for a TD Combo Buy Countdown Version I (Strict Version)

1. The close must be less than, or equal to, the low two price bars earlier;
2. Each TD Combo Buy Countdown low must be less than, or equal to, the low of the prior price bar;
3. Each TD Combo Buy Countdown close must be less than the previous TD Combo Buy Countdown close; and
4. Each TD Combo Buy Countdown close must be less than the close of the prior price bar.

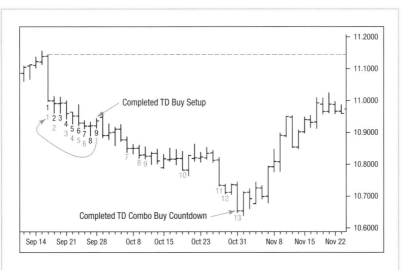

FIGURE 2.1   Complete TD Combo Buy Countdown Version I

In the chart of USDMXN, subsequent to the completion of TD Buy Setup, we go back to bar one and begin looking for the TD Combo Buy Countdown conditions from there onward.

Requirements for a TD Combo Buy Countdown Version II (Less-Strict Version)

The first four requirements are the same as for Version I:

1. The close must be less than, or equal to, the low two price bars earlier, up to and including bar ten of the TD Buy Countdown phase;

2. Each TD Combo Buy Countdown low must be less than, or equal to, the low of the prior price bar;

3. Each TD Combo Buy Countdown close must be less than the previous TD Combo Buy Countdown close; and

4. Each TD Combo Buy Countdown close must be less than the close of the prior price bar.

However, for TD Combo Buy Countdown bars eleven, twelve, and thirteen only,

5. The closes need only be successively lower, and it is not necessary to apply the more-stringent conditions listed earlier.

■ **To Enter a Long Position**

1. Wait for a successfully completed TD Combo Buy Countdown, and

2. Establish a long position on the close of bar thirteen.

■ **Risk Management: For Entering a TD Combo Buy Countdown Long Position**

1. Look for the bar that has the lowest true low within the TD Combo Buy Countdown process (every bar from one to thirteen inclusive, regardless of whether it is a numbered bar), and

2. Subtract the true range of that bar from its true low (**Figure 2.2**).

As they might with a TD Sequential Buy signal, more conservative traders, before entering a trade, can wait for the first price bar that has a close greater than the close four bars earlier, that is, a bullish TD Price Flip. This eliminates the risk of Recycling. Similar to the response to TD Sequential, a meaningful response can be expected within twelve price bars following the TD Combo Buy signal—ideally a bullish TD Price Flip and/or a move beyond the TD Reference Close (that is, a break of the highest high four bars prior to the low).

Rather than initiating a long position on the close of TD Combo Buy Countdown bar thirteen (my own personal preference), more conservative traders may prefer waiting for confirmation of a reversal from one of the following configurations: TD Camouflage, TD Clop, TD Clopwin, TD Open, or TD Trap.

The requirements for a TD Sell Setup within TD Combo are the same as those for a TD Sell Setup within TD Sequential.

■ **Requirements for a TD Combo Sell Setup Version I**

1. A Bullish TD Price Flip (that is, a close beneath the close four price bars earlier, immediately followed by a close above the close four price bars earlier), and

2. An uninterrupted series of nine closes, each one above the close four price bars earlier (starting from and inclusive of the Bullish TD Price Flip bar).

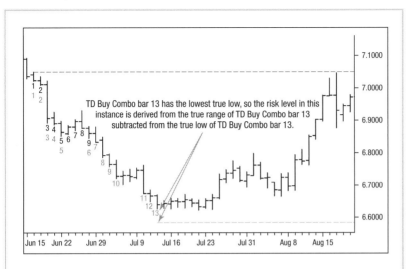

FIGURE 2.2   **Calculating the Risk Level Following a TD Combo Version I Buy Signal**

In the daily chart of USDSEK, a look at TD Countdown bars one to thirteen inclusive—including all bars, even those that aren't numbered—shows that TD Combo bar thirteen has the lowest true low. To calculate the TD risk level, we therefore take the true range of that bar and subtract that value from its true low.

Differences in Sell Countdown: TD Combo vs. TD Sequential

TD Combo Sell Countdown

Once the TD Combo Sell Setup is complete, the differences between TD Combo and TD Sequential manifest themselves:

TD Sequential waits for the termination of a TD Sell Setup and then begins looking for the conditions necessary to satisfy the requirements for a TD Sell Countdown,

But

TD Combo waits for a TD Sell Setup to complete, and then begins the TD Sell Countdown (from bar one of the preceding TD Sell Setup onward).

Commencing from bar one of the prior qualifying TD Sell Setup, the TD Sell Countdown phase of TD Combo begins retrospectively (**Figure 2.3**). Unlike TD Sequential, however, which simply requires

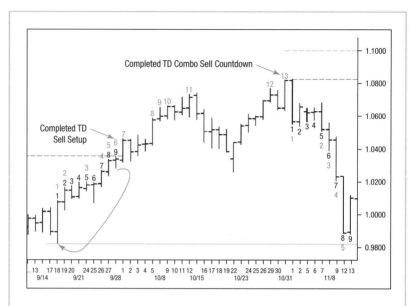

FIGURE 2.3   Complete TD Combo Sell Countdown Version I

In the daily chart of AUDCHF, subsequent to the completion of the TD Sell Setup, we go back to bar one and begin looking for the TD Combo Sell Countdown conditions from there onward.

that each close be greater than the corresponding high two price bars earlier, a TD Combo Sell requires that four conditions be satisfied simultaneously.

▣ Requirements for a TD Combo Sell Countdown Version I (More Strict)

The following conditions must be satisfied simultaneously:

1. The close must be greater than, or equal to, the high two price bars earlier;

2. Each TD Combo Sell Countdown high must be greater than, or equal to, the high of the previous price bar;

3. Each TD Combo Sell Countdown close must be greater than the close of the previous TD Combo Sell Countdown close; and

4. Each TD Combo Sell Countdown close must be greater than the close of the previous price bar.

TD Combo Sell Countdown Version II is very similar to Version I, but less strict.

Requirements for a TD Combo Sell Countdown Version II (Less Strict)

For Version II, as indicated below, the first four requirements are the same as for Version I, for TD Combo Sell Countdown bars one to ten inclusive:

1. The close must be greater than, or equal to, the high two price bars earlier;

2. Each TD Combo Sell Countdown high must be greater than, or equal to, the high of the previous price bar;

3. Each TD Combo Sell Countdown close must be greater than the close of the previous TD Combo Sell Countdown; and

4. Each TD Combo Sell Countdown close must be greater than the close of the previous price bar.

However, TD Combo Sell Countdown bars eleven, twelve, and thirteen only need to be successively higher, and it's not necessary to apply the more-stringent conditions listed above.

Risk Management: Calculating the Risk Level of a Short Position Following a TD Combo Sell Countdown

Following a successfully completed TD Combo Sell Countdown, the risk level for a short position may be calculated, and the trade established, on the close of bar thirteen:

1. Identify the bar that has the highest true high within the TD Combo Sell Countdown process (every bar from one to thirteen inclusive, as well as those that aren't numbered), and

2. Add the true range of that bar to its true high (**Figure 2.4**).

As they might with a TD Sequential Sell signal, more conservative traders can wait for the first price bar that has a close less than the close four bars earlier, that is, a bearish TD Price Flip, before entering a trade. This eliminates the risk of Recycling.

As you might with TD Sequential, you should expect a meaningful response within twelve price bars following the TD Combo Sell signal, ideally a bearish TD Price Flip and/or a move beyond the TD Reference Close, that is, a break of the lowest low four bars previous to the high.

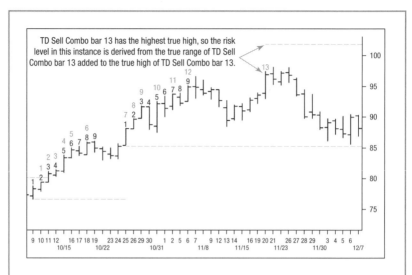

FIGURE 2.4 **Calculating the Risk Level Following a TD Combo Version I Sell Signal**

In the daily chart of Nymex crude oil (WTI), TD Countdown bars one to thirteen inclusive (including all bars whether numbered or not), TD Countdown bar thirteen has the highest true high. To calculate the TD risk level, we therefore take the true range of that bar and add that value to its true high.

Rather than initiating a short position on the close of TD Combo Sell Countdown bar thirteen, more-conservative traders may also want to wait for confirmation of a reversal after confirmation from TD Camouflage, TD Clop, TD Clopwin, TD Open, or TD Trap.

TD Combo Version I: Recommended Settings

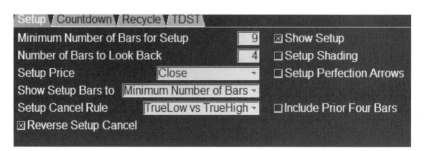

Countdown

☐ Show Countdown
Number of Bars for Countdown `13`   ☐ Countdown Completion Arrows
Number of Bars to Look Back `2`   ☐ Show Countdown Bars After Minimum
Termination Count `Close ▼`   Use 'Equal' for Comparison `All Bars ▼`
Countdown Price `Close ▼`
Show Risk Level `Use All Bars in Countdown ▼`

Buy Countdown Conditions
Countdown Price `<= ▼` Countdown Price 1 Bar Ago
Low `<= ▼` Low 1 Bar Ago

Sell Countdown Conditions
Countdown Price `>= ▼` Countdown Price 1 Bar Ago
High `>= ▼` High 1 Bar Ago

Recycle

☒ Reverse Setup Cancel   Recycle Count `18`
☒ Recycle Confirm   Recycle Setup Rule `Recycle All ▼`
☒ Enable Setup Within Setups   Recycle Multiplier `1.000` - `1.618`
Setup Within Setups Option 1 `Use Maximum Setup ▼`
Setup Within Setups Option 2 `Extreme Setup Closes Within True Range ▼`

TDST

☒ TDST On
☐ Extend the 2nd Most Recent TDST Level
☐ Open Restriction

CHAPTER **3**

TD D-Wave

"WHERE ARE WE GOING, and when will we get there?" impatient children ask their parents during a long journey; traders often ask me the same question about price action, when they're looking for insight into market direction and timing.

I find that Elliott wave theory addresses this question, and I am fortunate enough to work with some extremely good "Elliotticians." Nevertheless, while the Elliott wave theory appeals to me, I get frustrated by the subjective manner in which many people seem to apply it. As with politics, everyone has an opinion and a preferred Elliott wave count, but the opinions and counts aren't always objective or even rational, and are invariably dictated by preferred directional biases.

Fortunately, DeMark offers a solution to this problem. He saw merit in the Wave principle, but he decided to create rules, which he calls TD D-Wave, to insure objectivity in Elliott wave application and interpretation.

Unfortunately, DeMark didn't provide a detailed explanation of TD D-Wave. In fact, in his first book, *The New Science of Technical Analysis,* he devoted just a few pages to it, and he never referred to it again in any of his subsequent books. As a result, I field more questions about this particular study than any other TD indicator, with the possible exception of TD Sequential. I've lost track of the number of times someone has said to me, "I don't suppose you've written anything on the subject?" And so, in the interests of TD D-Wave *glasnost,* I will now give a more thorough explanation.

The Underlying Elliott Wave Principle

No discussion on TD D-Wave would be complete without first reviewing Elliott wave theory. So let's take a look at the underlying wave principle and then see how DeMark modified it to remove the more subjective elements.

Ralph Nelson Elliott, inspired by the writings of Charles Dow, developed his Elliott wave theory in the 1930s. The difference between his theory and Dow's can be summed up like this:

- **Dow** classified bull and bear trends in terms of accumulation and distribution phases between institutional and retail investors, but
- **Elliott** described markets in terms of three impulsive directional price movements (waves 1, 3, and 5), coupled with two separate nonimpulsive countertrend corrective moves (waves 2 and 4).

The Elliott wave's ensuing reversal unfolds in a sequence of three waves, two of which (waves A and C) are against what had been the dominant trend up until that point, and one of which (wave B) is in the direction of the previous trend.

To discern a trend, Dow Theory depends heavily on the relationship between previous price peaks and troughs (an uptrend is defined as a series of higher highs and higher lows, and a downtrend as a series of lower highs and lower lows). This approach is definitive, but it doesn't provide a great deal of insight into the timing of prospective turning points, since a trend reversal becomes apparent only after the fact.

Elliott wave, on the other hand, is more forward looking and, if used correctly, can significantly improve your chances of identifying price reversals before they happen.

As with TD Sequential, both Elliott wave and TD D-Wave are appealing because you can apply them to any market or time frame, regardless of the underlying volatility of the instrument in question, and without your needing to change any of the default indicator settings. If used properly, both Elliott wave and TD D-Wave can provide a roadmap to the direction of the market that you can use to determine price objectives and isolate prospective trend-exhaustion points.

Elliott Wave Basics

Familiarizing yourself with the behavioral characteristics of each wave will give you a better sense of where price action is, relative to the underlying trend at any given point. Let's look at the different stages of an uptrend (which can simply be reversed for a downtrend):

• **Wave 1** develops at a time when market sentiment is overwhelmingly bearish. Dow Theorists would classify this stage of the trend as the *accumulation phase*. Participation in this initial rally is limited, since economic news remains negative and investors are still inclined to sell rallies. At this point, "clued-up" institutional investors, acting on the premise that a tentative basing process is underway, tend to be the lone bulls and sole source of buying activity. Evidence that a broader basing process is developing manifests itself in the form of a) a threatening bullish divergence between price action and momentum, b) a price that is holding important trendline or Fibonacci supports, c) extreme sentiment readings, and d) declining open interest in the final stages of the prior decline.

• **Wave 2** invariably retraces a large part of wave 1's gains—at least 61.8 percent—but, crucially, cannot trade below the low of wave 1, where the original recovery began. During this pullback phase, bears try to reassert themselves, successfully wrestling into submission all but the strongest of bulls with the most conviction.

• **Wave3** is Elliott wave utopia, since it is the most powerful and impulsive stage of the advance (**Figure 3.2**). Open interest, volume, and price action should all pick up dramatically in the direction of the developing uptrend. More often than not, this phase starts gradually, as bulls try to gather momentum ahead of wave 1's peak. At this point, confidence in an upside resolution is relatively low, reflecting limited faith in the bulls' chances of successfully overcoming the high of wave 1. Sentiment shifts in favor of the upside, however, when wave 1's peak is eventually violated and short-covering, trend-follower involvement and institutional activity fuel fresh buying interest.

• **Wave 4** is the toughest time to trade, since price action during this phase tends to be volatile. The market typically retraces 38.2 percent of wave 3's gains, but can give back 61.8 percent or more, if wave 2 was very shallow. Trading during this phase can be extremely frustrating,

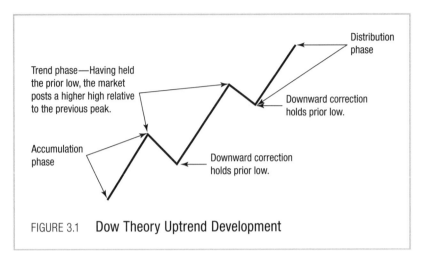

FIGURE 3.1   **Dow Theory Uptrend Development**

Distribution phase

Trend phase—Having held the prior low, the market posts a higher high relative to the previous peak.

Downward correction holds prior low.

Accumulation phase

Downward correction holds prior low.

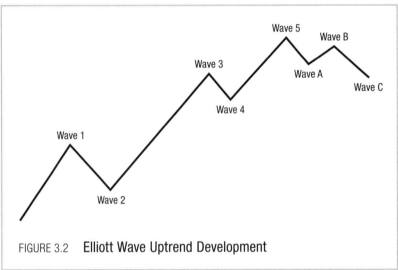

FIGURE 3.2   **Elliott Wave Uptrend Development**

Wave 5

Wave B

Wave 3

Wave A

Wave C

Wave 4

Wave 1

Wave 2

since profits on newly established trades can evaporate quickly and often turn into losses. Ideally, prices shouldn't dip back below the prior wave-1 high, but the low of wave 2 is the "line in the sand," since weakness beyond that point would invalidate the bullish wave count.

- **Wave 5** corresponds to the stage of the trend that Dow Theorists would recognize as full participation by the general public. The market continues to trade higher, and actually goes beyond the prior wave-3 peak (**Figure 3.1**). However, institutional buying interest dissipates in the latter stages of wave 5, as professional investors, recognizing that fresh long positions from current levels or higher are no longer favorable from a risk/reward perspective, become more defensive, and start taking protective measures in anticipation of a trend reversal. Early signs of a prospective top manifest themselves in the form of threatening (often pronounced), bearish divergence between price action and momentum.

- **Wave A** is what Dow Theorists would refer to as the "distribution phase." Economic news remains generally supportive of the broader uptrend, and sentiment indicators maintain a bullish bias, to the extent that the investing public views the setback as a healthy correction relative to what is still perceived as a strong uptrend.
- **Wave B** is also a difficult time to trade, as the attempted rally from the low of wave A fails to overcome the prior wave-5 peak.
- **Wave C** shares similar behavioral characteristics with wave 3. More often than not, this move lower is impulsive—breaking down into five Wave structures—and its length will tend to be 1.618 times that of wave A. Sentiment shifts from bullish to bearish when the market violates the prior wave A low and begins to form a series of lower highs and lower lows.

These basic aspects of Elliott wave make a lot of sense to me. What is troubling, however, is that most Elliotticians don't incorporate time into their analysis. Furthermore, while I have the good fortune to work with some of the most skilled and highly regarded Elliotticians in the business, who do an excellent job of interpreting the current wave count for me, I've always had difficulty figuring out a definitive Elliott wave count on my own. I particularly struggle when I'm trying to determine whether the market is in wave 3 or wave C or, at times, when wave 5 extends.

DeMark addressed the timing issue by introducing a set of definitive conditions that need to be satisfied in order to qualify each TD D-Wave—his "mechanized" version of Elliott wave.

DeMark's Mechanized Version of Elliott Wave

When applying TD D-Wave, the user has the option to select the high, low, or close for a reference price. DeMark originally recommended the high and low, but I prefer using the close instead, since, for the purposes of the TD D-Wave sequence, it is usually a more stable equilibrium level than intrabar price extremes. DeMark's timing rules define the minimum criteria necessary to complete each wave and initiate the next.

The Time Aspect of the TD D-Wave Requirements

One of the things I struggle with most in using Elliott wave is determining the timing for the origin of a Wave sequence. For TD D-Wave, in the case of an uptrend (reverse for a downtrend) the following is necessary.

■ TD D-Wave Requirements for Wave 1

To initiate an up-wave sequence,

1. The origin of the TD D-Wave up sequence is defined once the market records a twenty-one–bar–low close (a close less than all twenty prior closes).
2. Once condition one is satisfied, the market must post a thirteen-bar–high close (a close that is higher than all twelve prior closes). This confirms the origin of the TD D-Wave sequence and establishes that the market is in TD D-Wave 1.
3. TD D-Wave 1 is not considered complete, however, until price subsequently reaches an eight-bar–low close (a close less than all seven prior closes), which, in turn, confirms that TD D-Wave 2 is in progress.

■ TD D-Wave Requirements for Wave 2

1. The first requirement for wave 2 is the last requirement of wave 1, that is, that the market record an eight-bar–low close (a close less than all seven prior closes);

And then

2. TD D-Wave 2 continues until the market records a twenty-one–bar–high close (a close that is higher than all twenty previous closes), reinforcing the notion that TD D-Wave 3 is underway.

■ TD D-Wave Requirements for Wave 3

1. The first requirement of wave 3 is the last requirement of wave 2, that is, that TD D-Wave 2 continue until the market records a twenty-one-bar–high close

(a close that is higher than all twenty prior closes), reinforcing the notion that TD D-Wave 3 is underway;

And then

2. This remains the case until we see a thirteen-bar–low close (a close less than all twelve prior closes), thereby signaling that TD D-Wave 3 is complete and TD D-Wave 4 is unfolding.

■ TD D-Wave Requirements for Wave 4

1. The first requirement of wave 4 is the last requirement for wave 3, that is, that there be a thirteen-bar–low close (a close less than all twelve prior closes), thereby signaling that TD D-Wave 3 is complete and TD D-Wave 4 is developing;

And then

2. TD D-Wave 4 is considered complete when the market subsequently posts a thirty-four–bar–high close (a close greater than all thirty-three closes before it), representing the onset of TD D-Wave 5.

■ TD D-Wave Requirements for Wave 5

1. The first requirement for wave 5 is the last requirement for wave 4, that is, that there be a thirty-four-bar–high close (a close greater than all prior thirty-three closes), thereby signaling that TD D-Wave 4 is complete and TD D-Wave 5 is developing;

And then

2. TD D-Wave 5 is considered complete when the market subsequently posts a thirteen-bar–low close for TD D-Wave A (a close below all twelve prior closes), representing the onset of TD D-Wave A.

■ TD D-Wave Requirements for Wave A

1. The first requirement for wave A is the last requirement for wave 5, that is, that the market post a thirteen-bar–low close (a close less than all prior twelve closes), representing the onset of TD D-Wave A;

And then

2. TD D-Wave A is considered complete when the market subsequently posts an eight-bar–high close for TD D-Wave B (a close above all seven prior closes), representing the onset of TD D-Wave B.

■ TD D-Wave Requirements for Wave B

1. The first requirement for wave B is the last requirement for wave A, that is, an eight-bar–high close for TD D-Wave B (a close above all seven prior closes), representing the onset of TD D-Wave B;

And then

2. TD D-Wave B is considered complete when the market subsequently posts a twenty-one–bar–low close for TD D-Wave C (a close below all twenty prior closes), representing the onset of TD D-Wave C.

■ TD D-Wave Requirements for Wave C

1. The first requirement for wave C is the last requirement for wave B, that is, a twenty-one–bar–low close for TD D-Wave C (a close below all twenty prior closes), representing the onset of TD D-Wave C;

And then

2. TD D-Wave C is locked when the market closes below the low close of TD D-Wave A.

■ Additional Qualifying Rules for the Application of the TD D-Wave Indicators for an Uptrend

1. The peak close of TD D-Wave 3 must be higher than the peak close of TD D-Wave 1, and the peak close of TD D-Wave 5 must be above the peak close of TD D-Wave 3.

2. If a pullback from TD D-Wave 1 is so shallow that the decline fails to satisfy the conditions necessary to initiate TD D-Wave 2, and the market subsequently recovers above what had been the TD D-Wave 1 high close, then TD D-Wave 1 will shift over to the right in line with the new high close.

3. If a pullback from TD D-Wave 3 is so shallow that the decline fails to satisfy the conditions necessary to initiate TD D-Wave 4, and the market subsequently recovers above what had been the TD D-Wave 3 high close, then TD D-Wave 3 will shift to the right in line with the new high close.

4. If a pullback from TD D-Wave 5 is so shallow that the decline fails to satisfy the conditions necessary to initiate TD D-Wave A, and the market subsequently recovers above what had been the high close of TD D-Wave 5, then TD D-Wave 5 will shift over to the right in line with the new high close.

5. TD D-Wave 5 will be locked into place only when TD D-Wave C violates the low close of TD D-Wave A on a closing basis. Until that happens, if what had been TD D-Wave B closes above the high close of TD D-Wave 5, then TD D-Waves A and B will be erased, and TD D-Wave 5 will shift to the right.

6. If TD D-Wave 2 closes below the low close of TD D-Wave 1, then TD D-Wave 1 will disappear, and the count must begin anew. (Similarly, if the low close of TD D-Wave 4 closes below the low close of TD D-Wave 2, then TD D-Wave 2 will shift to where TD D-Wave 4 would otherwise have been.)

7. Once TD D-Wave C violates the low close of TD D-Wave A, TD D-Wave 5 is locked into place and cannot move. (Consequently, if the market subsequently closes back above the high close of TD D-Wave 5, rather than erasing TD D-Waves A, B, and C, and moving TD D-Wave 5 to the right, the indicator will instead label the move to new highs as a fresh TD D-Wave 1 advance rather than erasing the previous TD D-Wave 5.)

Additional Qualifiers for the Application of the TD D-Wave Indicators for a Downtrend

1. The trough of the low close of TD D-Wave 3 must be lower than the low close of TD D-Wave 1, and the trough of the low close of TD D-Wave 5 must be below the low close of TD D-Wave 3.

2. If a rebound from TD D-Wave 1 is so shallow that the advance fails to satisfy the conditions necessary to initiate TD D-Wave 2, and the market falls back below what had been the low close of TD D-Wave 1, then TD D-Wave 1 will shift to the right, in line with the new low close.

3. If a rally from TD D-Wave 3 is so shallow that the advance fails to satisfy the conditions necessary to initiate TD D-Wave 4, and the market falls back below what had been the low close of TD D-Wave 3, then TD D-Wave 3 will shift to the right, in line with the new low close.

4. If a rally from TD D-Wave 5 is so shallow that the rebound fails to satisfy the conditions necessary to initiate TD D-Wave A, and the market sells off below what had been the low close of TD D-Wave 5, then TD D-Wave 5 will shift to the right, in line with the new low close.

5. TD D-Wave 5 will be locked into place only when TD D-Wave C violates the high close of TD D-Wave A. Until that happens, if what had been TD D-Wave B trades below the low close of TD D-Wave 5, then TD D-Waves A and B will be erased, and TD D-Wave 5 will shift to the right.

6. If TD D-Wave 2 closes above the high close of TD D-Wave 1, then TD D-Wave 1 will disappear. (Similarly, if TD D-Wave 4 closes above the high close of TD D-Wave 2, then TD D-Wave 2 will shift to the right to where TD D-Wave 4 would otherwise have been.)

7. Once TD D-Wave C violates the high close of TD D-Wave A, TD D-Wave 5 is locked into place and cannot move. (Consequently, if the market subsequently closes back below the low close of TD D-Wave 5, rather than erasing TD D-Waves A, B, and C, and moving TD D-Wave 5 to the right, the indicator will instead label the move to new highs as a fresh TD D-Wave 1 advance.)

As with TD Sequential, TD D-Wave requires the market to dem-
onstrate that it is moving directionally by satisfying specific trending
criteria in order to categorize each wave. When prices are moving
laterally, TD D-Wave is silent, which means there is no need to try
to interpret the complex internal wave structure of a market that's
essentially going nowhere. When markets are confined to ranges for
a prolonged period of time, this aspect of TD D-Wave is particularly
helpful.

It is important to remember that, while TD D-Wave is similar
to Elliott wave, the two approaches do have their differences. An
Elliottician would be shocked, for example, to hear that TD D-Wave
breaks the cardinal Elliott rule, that wave must *not* be the shortest
wave. Although it is not a regular occurrence, there are situations in
TD D-Wave where TD D-Wave 3 *is* the shortest wave. Furthermore,
not only can TD D-Wave 4 *overlap* TD D-Wave 1's extreme, it can
even *violate the trough* of TD D-Wave 2 on an intrabar basis, as long as it
doesn't close beyond the extreme close of TD D-Wave 2.

Calculating TD D-Wave Projections

Personally, I'm interested in knowing only the projections for TD
D-Waves 3 (**Figure 3.3**) and 5 (**Figure 3.4**), but it is also possible to
determine objectives for TD D-Waves 2, 4, and C. Because I reference
closing prices, not highs and lows, to determine which wave the market
is in, I also prefer using closing prices to using highs or lows to project
future prices.

■ Bull Market Price Projections

TD D-Wave 1: Wait for a TD D-Wave 1 advance.

TD D-Wave 2: The TD D-Wave 2 pullback should ideally be 61.8 percent of the
distance traveled between the low close of TD D-Wave 1 and the high close of TD
D-Wave 1.

TD D-Wave 3: The TD D-Wave 3 upside objective is then determined by a) taking
the difference between the low close of TD D-Wave 1 and the high close of TD
D-Wave 1, b) multiplying that value by a factor of 1.618, and, then, c) adding that
result to the low close of TD D-Wave 1.

TD D-Wave 4: a) If TD D-Wave 2 was shallow, that is, in the region of 38.2 percent of TD D-Wave 1, then the expected retracement for TD D-Wave 4 would be

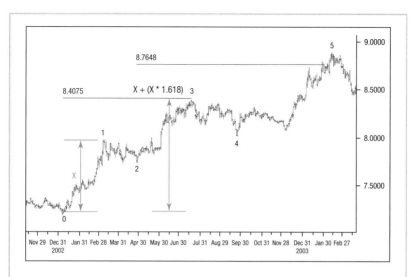

FIGURE 3.3   Upside Projection for TD D-Wave 3

The daily chart of EURNOK displays an upside projection for TD D-Wave 3. It is calculated by multiplying the difference between the low close of 0 and the high close of 1 by 1.618 and adding the result to the low close of 0.

FIGURE 3.4   Upside Projection for TD D-Wave 5

The daily chart of EURNOK displays an upside projection for TD D-Wave 5. It is calculated by multiplying the difference between the low close of 2 and the high close of 3 by 1.618 and adding the result to the low close of 2.

61.8 percent of the distance traveled between the low close of TD D-Wave 3 and the high close of TD D-Wave 3; but b) if TD D-Wave 2 was deep, that is, in the region of 61.8 percent of TD D-Wave 1, then the expected retracement for TD D-Wave 4 would be 38.2 percent of the distance traveled between the low close of TD D-Wave 3 and the high close of TD D-Wave 3.

TD D-Wave 5: a) Take the difference between the low close of TD D-Wave 3 and the high close of TD D-Wave 3; b) multiply it by a factor of 1.618; and c) add that value to the low close of TD D-Wave 3.

TD D-Wave C: a) Take the difference between the high close of TD D-Wave A and the low close of TD D-Wave A; b) multiply it by a factor of 1.618; and c) subtract that result from the high close of TD D-Wave A.

The Ultimate Targets for TD D-Waves 5 and C

DeMark's original explanation of the TD D-Wave projection focused on determining the ultimate targets for TD D-Waves 5 and C.

■ Upside Target for TD D-Wave 5

1. Take the difference between the low of TD D-Wave 1 and the high of TD D-Wave 1;
2. Multiply it by a factor of 1.382; and
3. Add the resulting value to the low of TD D-Wave 2 (noting that, if TD D-Wave 3 exceeds that level, then 2.764 should be substituted for the original 1.382 value).

■ Downside Target for Downside TD D-Wave C

1. Take the difference between the high of TD D-Wave A and the low of TD D-Wave A;
2. Subtract the result from the high of TD D-Wave B; and
3. Multiply that value by 1.618.

Bear Market Price Projections

Because I reference closing prices rather than highs and lows to determine which wave the market is in, I use closing prices, rather than highs or lows, for price projections (**Figures 3.6** and **3.7**).

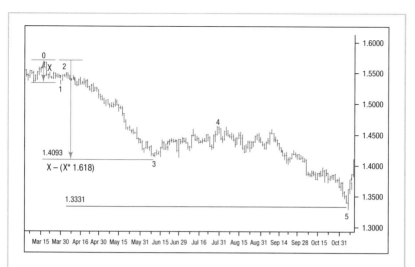

FIGURE 3.5 **Downside Projection for TD D-Wave 3**

The daily chart of EURCAD displays a downside projection for TD D-Wave 3. It is calculated by multiplying the difference between the high close of 0 and the low close of 1 by 1.618 and subtracting the result from the high close of 0.

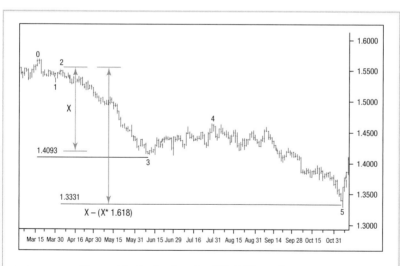

FIGURE 3.6 **Downside Projection for TD D-Wave 5**

The daily chart of EURCAD displays a downside projection for TD D-Wave 5. It is calculated by multiplying the difference between the high close of 2 and the low close of 3 by 1.618, and subtracting the result from the high close of 2.

■ Using Closing Prices for Price Projections

1. After a TD D-Wave 1 decline, the TD D-Wave 2 rebound should be 61.8 percent of the distance traveled between the high close of TD D-Wave 1 and the low close of TD D-Wave 1.

2. The ensuing TD D-Wave 3 downside objective is determined by a) taking the difference between the high close of TD D-Wave 1 and the low close of TD D-Wave 1, b) multiplying that value by a factor of 1.618, and then c) subtracting the result from the high close of TD D-Wave 1.

■ TD D-Wave 2: Shallow vs. Deep

If

TD D-Wave 2 was shallow, that is, in the region of 38.2 percent of TD D-Wave 1,

Then

The expected retracement for TD D-Wave 4 would be 61.8 percent of the distance traveled between the high close of TD D-Wave 3 and the low close of TD D-Wave 3.

If

TD D-Wave 2 was deep, that is, in the region of 61.8 percent of TD D-Wave 1,

Then

The expected retracement for TD D-Wave 4 would then be 38.2 percent of the distance traveled between the high close of TD D-Wave 3 and the low close of TD D-Wave 3.

■ To Calculate the Objective for TD D-Wave 5

1. Take the difference between the high close of TD D-Wave 3 and the low close of TD D-Wave 3,

2. Multiply that by a factor of 1.618, and

3. Subtract that value from the high close of TD D-Wave 3.

■ To Calculate TD D-Wave C

1. Take the difference between the low close of TD D-Wave A and the high close of TD D-Wave A,

2. Multiply that by a factor of 1.618, and

3. Add that value to the low close of TD D-Wave A.

As mentioned above, DeMark's original explanation of the TD D-Wave projection focused on determining the ultimate targets for TD D-Waves 5 and C. Here are his thoughts:

- ## To Determine the Eventual Downside Objective for TD D-Wave 5

    1. Take the difference between the high of TD D-Wave 1 and the low of TD D-Wave 1;

    2. Multiply that by a factor of 1.382; and

    3. Subtract the result from the high of TD D-Wave 2 (noting that, if TD D-Wave 3 exceeds that level, then 2.764 should be substituted for the original 1.382 value).

- ## To Determine the Upside Objective for TD D-Wave C

    1. Take the difference between the low of TD D-Wave A and the high of TD D-Wave A,

    2. Add the result to the low of TD D-Wave B, and

    3. Multiply that value by 1.618.

TD D-Wave Frequently Asked Questions

Most of the time, two alternate TD D-Wave counts are evident—a bullish and a bearish scenario. How do I differentiate objectively between the two possibilities, to arrive at a preferred directional TD D-Wave count?

This is an issue I struggled with for quite some time, but I found that combining TD D-Wave with a momentum-based oscillator like Welles Wilder's Relative Strength Index (RSI) can result in an objective, directional conclusion.

- ## The Relative Strength Index

    The RSI is one of the few non-DeMark indicators I use in conjunction with the TD studies. The indicator takes the prior fourteen periods and compares the strength of the up and down moves over that period to figure out whether the bulls or bears are in control of price action. Averaging the up and down moves between bars on a closing basis over that time results in the Relative Strength (RS). The information can be translated into index form (RSI), calibrated between zero and one hundred, using the formula $RSI = 100 \, [100/1 + RS]$.

The majority of traders use oscillators to identify prospective overbought or oversold situations or to highlight divergences between

---

The RSI was presented in 1978 by Welles Wilder, in his book *New Concepts in Technical Trading Systems*.

momentum and price action, but that approach is flawed, because the RSI is calibrated between zero and one hundred, and, in a strong uptrend, for example, the market typically doesn't enter extreme oversold territory during a corrective down move. Furthermore, an extreme overbought reading is often associated with strong buying interest, rather than upside trend exhaustion.

Combining the RSI with TD D-Wave, on the other hand, helps to put both the TD D-Wave sequence and the corrective price action into context relative to the broader trend. During the early stages of a trend (particularly TD D-Wave 1), it is fairly common for the RSI to become overextended, and not unusual for multiple divergence signals to manifest themselves, possibly making traders wary about sticking with the developing trend.

The RSI, however, after being overbought or oversold for a prolonged period of time in the direction of the underlying trend, will often revert to a mildly overbought or oversold state. In doing so, it regains its composure ahead of a resumption of the broader developing trend. If we could isolate these turns in momentum, TD D-Wave interpretation would be much clearer, which would be a distinct advantage.

Typically, overbought and oversold RSI zones are set at seventy-five and twenty-five respectively. This is all well and good when markets are confined to ranges, but, for reasons stated earlier, it is less helpful when prices are trending directionally. If additional thresholds are incorporated at forty and sixty, respectively, however, the moderate corrections referred to above become more apparent.

Broadly speaking, if the market is advancing as part of a bullish TD D-Wave up sequence, then the RSI should remain above forty during corrective setbacks for TD D-Waves 2 and 4 (**Figure 3.7**).

Similarly, if the market is declining as part of a bearish TD D-Wave down sequence, then the RSI should remain beneath sixty during corrective rallies for TD D-Waves 2 and 4 (**Figure 3.8**).

Since we also know that TD D-Waves should not overlap (in an uptrend for example, the low close of TD D-Wave 4 should not be less than the low close of TD D-Wave 2, and the low close of TD D-Wave 2 should not be below the low close for the origin of TD D-Wave 1), it should be possible to isolate acute risk/reward trading opportunities that coincide with the termination of each corrective

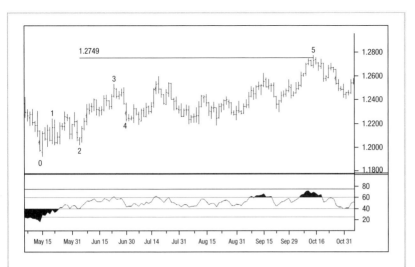

FIGURE 3.7   Uptrend: TD D-Wave Combined with the Relative
Strength Indicator

In the daily chart of USDCHF, note how setbacks in the broad uptrend find support at the
RSI level of forty, thereby biasing the count to the bullish side.

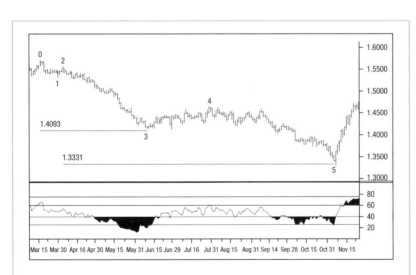

FIGURE 3.8   Downtrend: TD D-Wave Combined with the Relative
Strength Indicator

In the daily chart of EURCAD, note how rallies in the broad downtrend find resistance
at the RSI level of sixty, thereby biasing the count to the bearish side.

move, particularly if the expected termination of each corrective move is accompanied by a TD Sequential or a TD Combo buy signal—either a TD Buy Setup or a TD Buy Countdown.

Let's take a look at how this fits with price action in more practical terms, as a trend unfolds:

- **When a strong bull market is underway,** TD D-Wave price corrections ought to find support at the RSI sixty level, while deeper TD D-Wave price setbacks should be underpinned by the RSI forty level.
- **When a strong bear market is underway,** TD D-Wave corrective price recoveries ought to find resistance at the RSI forty level, while larger-degree TD D-Wave price rebounds should be rebuffed by the RSI sixty level.
- **When a price setback in a bull market is sufficiently strong to violate support at the RSI forty level** (particularly when that level has held for a prolonged period of time), it's often a precursor of a reversal of the broader trend and a switch from a bullish to a bearish TD Wave structure.
- **When a price recovery in a bear market is sufficiently strong to violate resistance at the RSI sixty level** (particularly when that level has held for a prolonged period of time), it's often a precursor of a reversal of the broader trend and a switch from a bearish to a bullish TD Wave structure.
- **To determine TD D-Wave 5 peaks and troughs,** use of the RSI can be extremely helpful, since these invariably diverge from the price peaks or troughs of TD D-Wave 3. This divergence results in what is commonly known as a *failure swing*, whereby the price posts a new high relative to the previous market top, or a new low relative to the previous trough in the market—but the corresponding RSI value fails to exceed the previous high (during an uptrend), or go below the previous low (during a downtrend).
- **When no failure swing is apparent,** it's often a reflection of the fact that the underlying trend is very powerful, and a TD D-Wave extension, rather than a reversal, is likely.

How should I trade the TD D-Wave sequence?

- Initiate positions on the break of the TD D-Wave 1 extreme, in line with the underlying trend, since this reinforces the notion that the market is likely to be in the impulsive TD D-Wave 3 directional phase;

- Remain on the sidelines, or follow a short-term scalping approach, not looking for directional moves during TD D-Wave 4;
- Establish positions in the direction of the dominant trend as price breaks the extreme of TD D-Wave 3 when the market is in TD D-Wave 5; and
- Initiate countertrend trades at the end of TD D-Waves 5 and B.

Some of the advice above is simply stating the obvious. What additional advantage is there for me in using TD D-Wave?
You *can* use the study in isolation, but I would suggest combining it with other TD indicators, such as TD Sequential and/or TD Combo. While TD D-Wave defines prospective price targets and helps to determine the stage of the trend price action, TD Sequential and TD Combo isolate potential price-exhaustion levels. I believe this application of the indicators is more valuable than simply waiting for the extremes of TD D-Waves 1 and 3 to break, in order to put a directional trade on. Remember, the Bloomberg terminal indicates (with an arrow) when the minimum criteria for the completion of each TD D-Wave have been satisfied. If that arrow happens to coincide with a completed TD Sequential Countdown, TD Combo Countdown signal, or a situation in which the market completes a TD Setup ahead of a TDST level, it often presents an acute risk/reward trading opportunity. In fact, the optimum times to trade are when any of these signals coincides with the satisfaction of the minimum conditions for TD D-Wave 2 or TD D-Wave B. Rather than waiting for confirmation, if you can identify the start of TD D-Wave 3 or the beginning of TD D-Wave C, you will have a distinct advantage over other traders. Being able to isolate the prospective origin of TD D-Wave 3 is particularly useful when you are trading options.

For example, prior to TD D-Wave 3 up's overcoming TD D-Wave 1, the broader market doesn't recognize the reversal yet. Most traders believe that TD D-Wave 1 is an anomaly and that the setback in TD D-Wave 2 will exceed the origin of TD D-Wave 1, thereby reinstating the broader down trend. Often, the risk reversal on options (which measures the market's preference for puts or calls relative to the underlying instrument) favors the downside at this point, and, if TD D-Wave 2 has not been particularly choppy, option volatility will also be quite low.

For those who like to trade TD signals via options, the best opportunity is at the prospective start of TD D-Wave 3. If you're correct and you manage to catch the end of TD D-Wave 2, you benefit from the "double whammy" of increased volatility when price clears the high of TD D-Wave 1 and of the directional implications of being involved in a trend before it turns impulsive.

Discerning whether the market is in Wave C or Wave 3 is also a challenge for Elliotticians. If, following what you think is a Wave 2 pullback, you trade the break of what would be Wave 1's extreme, thinking a trend reversal is underway, and it turns out to be Wave C rather than wave 3, you end up either selling near the low or buying near the top of an exhaustive move up. The advantage of combining TD D-Wave with TD Sequential or TD Combo, then, is that you can identify prospective trend reversals early on. Of course, there's still a risk that you might be seeing TD D-Wave C and not TD D-Wave 3, but that doesn't matter so much if you act early.

Both TD D-Wave C and TD D-Wave 3 have the same directional implications—it's just a question of magnitude. TD D-Wave C posts a marginal and unsustainable break of TD D-Wave A's extreme, whereas TD D-Wave 3 has an impulsive break of the TD D-Wave 1 price extreme. For this reason, if, rather than waiting for the break of TD D-Wave 1 or TD D-Wave A for confirmation of a change in direction, you initiate a position at the start of TD D-Wave C or TD D-Wave 3, you can trail your stop-loss to entry when the extreme price of TD D-Wave A or TD D-Wave 1 is violated.

I can see how removing internal counts reduces confusion when markets are trading in a wide and choppy range for a prolonged period of time, but, if I don't try to do that, how do I figure out the bigger or smaller picture?

Remember, TD D-Wave is based on relative price action, and so, if you particularly want to see TD D-Wave counts of a higher or lower degree, you simply apply the study to a longer or shorter time frame. I find looking at longer time frames particularly helpful, because it enables me to discern whether a price move is an impulse—or a corrective wave relative to the bigger picture. Trends are likely to be extremely impulsive if a market is in TD D-Wave 3 on a daily, weekly, and monthly basis, for example. Imagine how powerful that information could be if you were able to identify the start of the move with TD Sequential and/or TD Combo.

From a longer-term positioning perspective, it's also helpful to know on a daily, weekly, and monthly basis when a market is in TD D-Wave 5, since that information provides an invaluable insight into prospects for the broader trend and on the proper positioning for more acute directional trading opportunities from a risk/reward perspective.

The first instance in which TD D-Wave 3 lines up in multiple time frames is when a trader should express views more forcefully in terms of leveraged positioning.

The first instance in which TD D-Wave 5 is confirmed in multiple time frames is when longer-term traders, who had been positioned in the direction of what had been the broader trend up until that point, should begin to reduce their market exposure. At the very least, they should purchase some protection for the underlying position in antici-pation of a broader trend reversal.

Can I experiment with different numbers for the TD D-Wave qualifiers?
Yes, you can, as long as the number of bars in your sequence maintains the same ratio relationships as the recommended twenty-one–, thirteen–, eight–, twenty-one–, thirteen–, thirty-four–, thirteen–, eight–, and twenty-one–bar sequence.

TD D-Wave: Recommended Settings

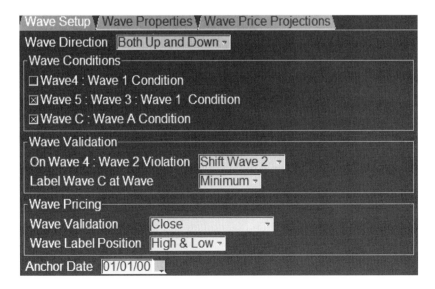

Wave Setup	Wave Properties	Wave Price Projections

| Up Waves Color | Cyan ▾ |
| Down Waves Color | Yellow ▾ |

Wave	Level
0	21
1	13
2	8
3	21
4	13
5	34
A	13
B	8
C	21

Wave Setup	Wave Properties	Wave Price Projections

No.	On	From	To	Times	Direction	At	Stop	Color
1	☒	0 ▾	1 ▾	1.618	Up ▾	0 ▾	3 ▾	Cyan ▾
2	☒	2 ▾	3 ▾	1.618	Up ▾	2 ▾	5 ▾	Cyan ▾
3	☒	0 ▾	1 ▾	1.618	Down ▾	0 ▾	3 ▾	Yellow ▾
4	☒	2 ▾	3 ▾	1.618	Down ▾	2 ▾	5 ▾	Yellow ▾

CHAPTER 4

TD Lines

ONE OF THE SIMPLEST and most widely used technical-analysis tools is the humble trendline, but, ironically, this cornerstone of research sits on rocky foundations. Give a room full of people the same price chart, and ask them to insert trendlines on it, and you can be sure of two things: 1) that everyone will draw something completely different, and 2) that, more often than not, the trendlines will be constructed based on subjective, directional biases rather than sound, objective reasoning. (No prizes for guessing, for example, the bullish or bearish preferences of someone who opts to draw an upward-sloping channel.)

DeMark's approach to the construction of trendlines may not be conventional, but it is certainly objective and completely removes wishful thinking from the decision-making process. As with many other TD indicators, DeMark's trendline theory can be practically applied to any market or time frame, and so the methodology is equally relevant whether you are day trading or position trading.

The key to drawing trendlines objectively is selecting the right points. DeMark contends that the most significant points to connect are pivot points, that is, levels that coincide with trend reversals. A low surrounded on either side by higher lows is significant, as is a high bordered by lower highs. DeMark refers to these levels as *TD Points*, and the lines connecting them as *TD Lines*. Their significance is determined by the number of surrounding highs and lows. For example, a high that has five lower highs on either side of it is labeled a *Level Five TD Supply Point*, while a low with three higher lows on either side of

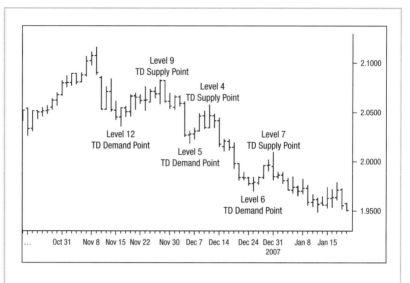

FIGURE 4.1   **TD Points**

A high with seven lower highs on either side of it is a Level Seven TD Supply Point,
while a low with six higher lows on either side of it is a Level Six TD Demand Point.

it is a *Level Three TD Demand Point*. You can select TD Points (**Figure 4.1**) of any level to construct TD Lines, but my personal preference is Level One TD Lines, since they are more responsive to price action than higher-level TD Points, and therefore provide an earlier breakout signal. That said, it is worth monitoring TD Lines on multiple time frames and/or TD Lines on different levels, since breakouts are more likely to be significant when clustered lines give way simultaneously.

Unlike the trendlines in traditional technical analysis, which require a minimum of three points to construct, a TD Line needs only two reference points. Furthermore, in recognition of the fact that markets are dynamic and that recent price action is arguably more significant than price action further in the past, TD Lines are drawn from right to left, rather than left to right, using the two most recent TD Points. To determine support, connect the two most recent TD Demand Points of the same magnitude (from right to left) to draw an upward–sloping TD Demand Line. To determine resistance, connect the two most recent TD Supply Points of the same magnitude (from right to left) to draw a downward–sloping TD Supply Line (**Figure 4.2**).

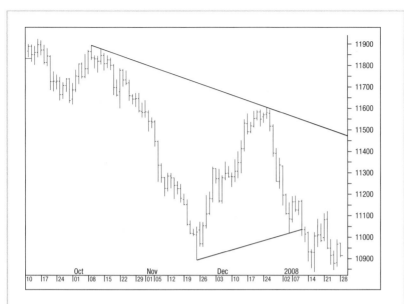

FIGURE 4.2 **TD Lines**

Connecting the most-recent Level Three TD Demand Point with the next-most-recent, lower Level Three TD Demand Point results in a Level Three TD Demand Line. Connecting the most-recent Level Three TD Supply Point with the next-most-recent, higher Level Three TD Supply Point results in a Level Three TD Supply Line.

TD Demand Points and TD Supply Lines are constantly being redefined as new TD Demand Points and TD Supply Points appear, insuring that they adapt dynamically as price action unfolds.

Having determined how to construct TD Demand Lines and TD Supply Lines, DeMark developed a set of rules about how prices should respond to these levels. He observed that unexpected trendline violations often overshoot in the direction of the break, as stop-losses are triggered and trend followers or breakout traders exaggerate the move in the near term.

Conversely, short-term breakouts tend to not follow through immediately on trendline violations that have been widely anticipated, since traders have those positions on ahead of the break. DeMark's rules distinguish between qualified, or solid, trendlines and disqualified, or broken, trendlines, and so traders can initiate fresh positions in the direction of a qualified intrabar break—and fade moves when a disqualified intrabar violation occurs. This insight is particularly useful, because conventional technical analysis argues one should wait for the violation of a trendline on a closing basis before entering a position in the direction of the breakout.

The Three TD Demand Line Qualifiers

Once you've constructed a TD Demand Line, each one of the following three conditions (**Figure 4.3**) needs to be taken into account to determine whether initiating a fresh trade in the direction of the break is warranted, prior to the close. As long as one or more of the conditions are satisfied, an intrabar trendline break is expected, and a closing violation beyond the breakout level is likely.

■ TD Demand Line Qualifier Condition One

Assuming the price bar that violates a TD Demand Line to the downside is called *bar X*, you need to compare the close of X − 1 (that is, the price bar prior to the downside breakout) with the close of X − 2 (that is, the close two price bars before the downside breakout).

If

The close of X − 1 is higher than the close of X − 2,

Then

There's a reasonable chance that bar X will close beneath TD Demand Line support.

The logic for this reasoning is that, if a higher close occurs prior to a downside break of a TD Demand Line, market participants are predisposed to thinking that upward momentum will continue, and near-term buying pressure persists. Consequently, when prices break lower unexpectedly, bulls are forced to stop out of long positions, while bears establish fresh shorts, thereby increasing the likelihood of a close below TD Demand Line support.

Conversely, if we have a lower close the bar before a downside violation of a TD Demand Line, that intrabar break is less likely to be sustained on a closing basis, since short-term traders were already positioned for the move in anticipation of further weakness. Practically speaking, this means that, if there is an up close the bar before a

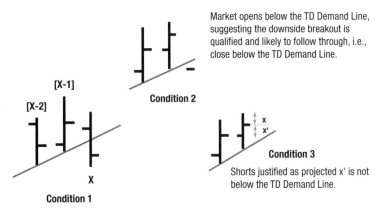

Market opens below the TD Demand Line, suggesting the downside breakout is qualified and likely to follow through, i.e., close below the TD Demand Line.

Condition 2

[X-1]

[X-2]

Condition 1

X

Condition 3

Shorts justified as projected x' is not below the TD Demand Line.

Close of bar [X-1] is higher than the close of bar [X-2] for the period prior to the breakout, so the intrabar downside violation of the TD Demand Line is qualified, justifying short entry on the break of the trendline rather than having to wait for the close for confirmation.

FIGURE 4.3   **The Three Different Conditions That Would Produce a Valid TD Demand Line Break**

downside break of a TD Demand Line, then you can sell on the break of the TD Demand Line, expecting a close below it.

If you see a down close the bar before a downside violation of a TD Demand Line, then you can fade the intrabar TD Demand Line break, expecting the market to close back above it.

■ TD Demand Line Qualifier Condition Two

If

The price opens below a TD Demand Line,

Then

It indicates that new selling pressure has shifted the near-term supply/demand dynamic in favor of the bears, meaning that the break would be considered a qualified violation of support in TD terms, and you could therefore sell on the break of the TD Demand Line, expecting the market to close below it.

Assuming that neither of the first two conditions is satisfied, you can use one final qualifier to measure selling pressure, that is, supply, ahead of a TD Demand Line downside breakout.

▪ TD Demand Line Qualifier Condition Three

1. Assuming a breakout bar *X*, identify the price bar before the TD Demand Line downside violation (X − 1), and calculate the difference between that bar's close and the greater of either a) that bar's high or b) the previous bar's close (close of X − 2); and

2. Subtract that value from the close of X − 1.

If

The resulting number is *above* the TD Demand Line,

Then

Sell on the intrabar break of the TD Demand Line, expecting the market to close below it.

If

The number is *below* the TD Demand Line support,

Then

The intrabar break is considered disqualified, and is less likely to follow through to the upside on a closing basis; that is, you can fade the move intrabar.

Calculating the Objective for a TD Demand Line Break

You'll recall from Physics 101 that every action has an equal and opposite reaction. But it is DeMark's contention that this law of motion isn't confined to the science lab, that it can also be applied to markets, and that there is often some symmetry in markets. What happens in terms of price action above a TD Demand Line is often replicated below it, following a qualified downside break (**Figure 4.4**).

▪ To Determine the Objective for a Qualified Downside Violation

1. Identify the highest true high above the TD Demand Line, and drop a perpendicular line to the corresponding TD Demand Line below it.

2. Subtract that value from the point where the qualified breakout occurred.

The objective remains intact unless the market has a qualified breakout to the upside—in which case the supply/demand dynamics will have shifted, or the downside trendline breakout target will have been reached.

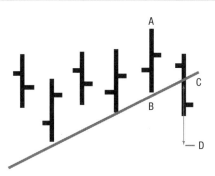

FIGURE 4.4   Calculating the Downside Objective for a TD Demand
Line Break

Identify the highest true high above the TD Demand Line (Point A), and drop a perpendicular line to the corresponding TD Demand Line below it (Point B). Subtract the
value of the perpendicular line (A − B) from the point at which the qualified breakout
occurs (Point C), which gives you the projected downside target (Point D).

Now, having entered a short position following a qualified intrabar
downside break of a TD Demand Line, you need some rules to get
you out of that position if things don't play out according to plan.

▦ Exiting a Short Position Using TD Demand Line

There are three guidelines for closing out a short trade following an unsuccessful
break of a TD Demand Line:

1. If the open of the bar immediately after the downside breakout is above the
   TD Demand Line breakout level, exit at the open.

2. If the open of the bar immediately after the downside breakout is above the
   TD Demand Line, and the bar closes above the TD Demand Line breakout level,
   exit at the close.

3. If the low of the bar following the TD Demand Line break fails to record a lower
   low than the low of the breakout bar, exit at the close.

TD Supply Line Qualifiers

Once you've constructed a TD Supply Line, each one of the following
three conditions (**Figure 4.5**) needs to be taken into account to determine whether or not initiating a fresh long position in the direction of

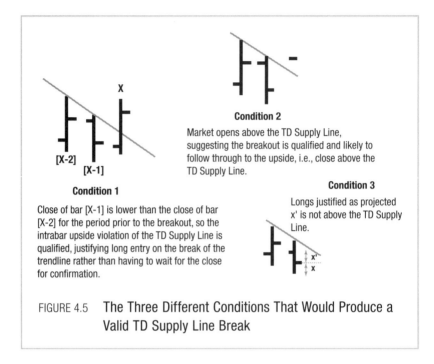

Condition 2

Market opens above the TD Supply Line, suggesting the breakout is qualified and likely to follow through to the upside, i.e., close above the TD Supply Line.

Condition 1

Close of bar [X-1] is lower than the close of bar [X-2] for the period prior to the breakout, so the intrabar upside violation of the TD Supply Line is qualified, justifying long entry on the break of the trendline rather than having to wait for the close for confirmation.

Condition 3

Longs justified as projected x' is not above the TD Supply Line.

FIGURE 4.5   **The Three Different Conditions That Would Produce a Valid TD Supply Line Break**

the break is warranted prior to the close. As long as one or more of the conditions is satisfied, an intrabar trendline break is expected and a closing violation beyond the breakout level is likely.

◼ Initiation of a Fresh Long Position Qualifier One

Assuming the price bar that violates a TD Supply Line to the upside is bar X, you need to compare the close of $X - 1$ (that is, the bar prior to the upside breakout) with the close of $X - 2$ (that is, the close two bars before the upside breakout).

If the close of $X - 1$ is lower than the close of $X - 2$, then there's a reasonable chance that bar X will close above TD Supply Line resistance.

The logic for this reasoning is that, if a lower close occurs prior to an upside break of a TD Supply Line, market participants are predisposed to thinking that downward momentum will continue and near-term selling pressure will persist. Consequently, when prices break higher unexpectedly, bears are forced to stop out of short positions, while bulls establish fresh longs, thereby increasing the likelihood of a close above TD Supply Line resistance. Conversely, if a higher close occurs the bar before an upside violation of a TD Supply Line, that intrabar break is less likely to be sustained on a closing basis, since short-term traders will have already been positioned for the down move in anticipation of further weakness. Practically speaking, this means that, if you see a down that closes the bar before an upside break of a TD Supply Line, you can buy on the break of the TD Supply Line, expecting a close above it.

If you see an up close the bar before an upside violation of a TD Supply Line, you can fade the intrabar break of the TD Supply Line, expecting the market to close back below it.

■ Initiation of a Fresh Long Position Qualifier Two

If a price opens above a TD Supply Line, it indicates that new buying pressure has shifted the near-term supply/demand dynamic in favor of the bulls. As such, the break would be deemed to be a qualified violation of resistance in TD terms, and you could therefore buy on the break of the TD Supply Line, expecting the market to close above it.

Assuming neither of the first two conditions is satisfied, you can use one final qualifier to measure buying pressure, that is, demand ahead of a TD Supply Line upside breakout (**Figure 4.6**).

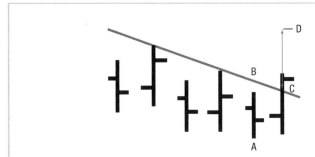

FIGURE 4.6   Calculating the Upside Objective for a TD Supply Line Break

Identify the lowest true low below the TD Supply Line (Point A), and extend a perpendicular line up to corresponding TD Supply Line above it (Point B). Add the value of the perpendicular line (B − A) to the point at which the qualified breakout occurs (Point C), which results in the projected upside target (Point D).

Initiation of a Fresh Long Position Qualifier Three

Assuming a breakout bar *X*, look at the price bar before the TD Supply Line upside violation (X − 1).

1. Calculate the difference between that bar's close and the lower of that bar's low or the previous bar's close (the close of X − 2), and

2. Add that value to the close of X − 1.

If

The resulting number is *below* the TD Supply Line,

Then

Buy on the intrabar break of the TD Supply Line, expecting the market to close above it.

But if

The number is *above* the TD Supply Line resistance,

Then

The intrabar break is considered disqualified and less likely to follow through to the downside on a closing basis; that is, you can fade the move intrabar.

Calculating the Objective for a TD Supply Line Break

To determine the objective for a qualified upside violation,

1. Identify the lowest true low below the TD Supply Line, and draw a perpendicular line up to the corresponding TD Supply Line above it.

2. Add the value of the perpendicular line to the point where the qualified breakout occurred.

The objective will remain intact unless the market has a qualified downside breakout—in which case the supply/demand dynamics will have shifted, or the upside trendline breakout target will have been reached.

Having entered a long position following a qualified intrabar upside break of a TD Supply Line, you need some rules to get you out of that position if things don't play out according to plan.

TD Supply Line and Exiting a Long Position

There are three opportunities for closing out a short trade following an unsuccessful upside break of a TD Supply Line.

1. If the open of the bar immediately after the upside breakout is below the TD Supply Line breakout level, exit at the open.

2. If the open of the bar immediately after the upside breakout is below the TD Supply Line, and the bar closes below the TD Supply Line breakout level, exit at the close.

3. If the high of the bar following the TD Supply Line break fails to post a higher high than the high of the breakout bar, exit at the close.

This objective approach to trendline construction proves that you can remove subjective directional biases from the decision-making process. Applying definitive rules to the identification of TD Demand Points and TD Supply Points, determining whether breakouts are qualified or disqualified, and having a clear methodology for determining TD Line breakout targets should help you time the market and improve your trading consistency. Furthermore, since this approach enables you to act preemptively intrabar ahead of a closing break, it can, over time, reduce slippage on trades. (By way of an aside, some people apply trendlines to momentum oscillators. Using the logic outlined here for TD Lines, you can experiment with applying TD Lines to overbought/oversold indicators, to determine qualified/disqualified breaks and projections for qualified breakouts. Since momentum is a derivative of price, ideally you would want to see a price and momentum trendline simultaneously giving way from overbought/oversold territory.)

TD Lines: Recommended Settings

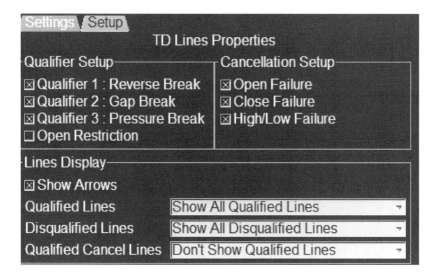

Settings Setup

TD Lines Properties

Level for TD Points   1
Max # of times to use TD Point   10
Bars to Look Back   400
Price Projection Calculation %   100.0
☒ Use True High/True Low
☐ TD Line Confirm

CHAPTER 5

TD Retracements

As WITH THE CONSTRUCTION OF TRENDLINES, the application of Fibonacci retracement levels is a highly subjective process. Traders will invariably select highs and lows based on what they perceive to be critical price levels, and so it is hardly surprising that different peaks and troughs have various importance, depending on the role of the market participants.

DeMark found that the most objective way to determine which reference high to use when projecting retracements from a reference low was to determine when the market last traded at the reference low, and then choose the highest point between the two lows.

Conversely, to determine which reference low to use when projecting retracements from a reference high, determine when the market last traded at the reference high, and select the lowest point between the two highs.

DeMark refers to this method, as well as its associated ratios 0.382 and 0.618, *TD Magnet Price*, and associated ratios 1.382, 1.618, 2.236, and 2.618 as *TD Relative Retracement* (**Figures 5.1** and **5.2**).

■ Determining References for Projecting TD Relative Retracements
If you're anticipating a down move subsequent to a rally,
1. Calculate the difference between the reference high and reference low;
2. Multiply that number by 0.382 and 0.618, and
3. Subtract the resulting values from the reference high.

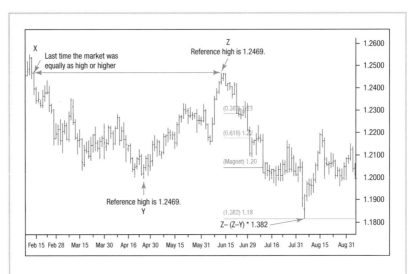

FIGURE 5.1   Downside TD Relative Retracement

In the daily chart of USDCHF, the downside TD Relative Retracement levels are calculated by determining when the market last traded above the reference high, then selecting the lowest point between the two highs. The resulting value is then multiplied by
Fibonacci ratios, 0.382 and 0.618, 1.382, and so forth. The results are then subtracted
from the reference high. In this instance, the high reference price is 1.2469 on June 14,
2007. The last time the market was equally as high or higher is February 14, 2007. The
lowest point in between is on April 25. Note how the 1.382 projection of that move cuts
in at 1.1816. The low on August 8 is 1.1817, before the market bounces to 1.2215.

If you're expecting an up move subsequent to a decline,

1. Calculate the difference between the reference low and reference high;

2. Multiply that number by 0.382 and 0.618, and

3. Add the resulting values to the reference low.

If the market closes above the 0.382 retracement, there's a reasonable chance that it will extend to the 0.618 retracement level. If it
closes above the 0.618 retracement level, it's likely that the market will
extend even higher, to the TD Magnet Price.

The TD Magnet Price is important, because most people concentrate their attention on the 1.00 retracement, that is, the extreme
high or low of the reference level—once the 0.618 level is breached.

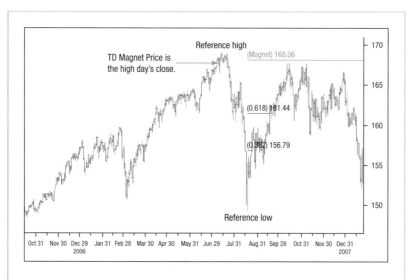

FIGURE 5.2   Upside TD Relative Retracement Levels

In the daily chart of EURJPY, the upside TD Relative Retracement levels are calculated by determining when the market last traded below the reference low, and then selecting the highest point between the two lows. The resulting value is multiplied by 0.382 and 0.618, and the results are then added to the reference low. Note how the TD Magnet Price (the close of the high reference day) provides resistance on a number of occasions.

DeMark's research, however, suggests that prices are instead often drawn to the reference high bar's close or the reference low bar's close, rather than the intrabar price extreme. It is because prices are drawn to the close of the reference high or reference low that DeMark refers to this level as the TD Magnet Price. He concluded that, more often than not, prices respond to this level, rather than to the reference high or reference low.

Failure at the TD Magnet Price tends to lead to a resumption of the broader trend, while a successful break of the TD Magnet Price tends to lead to a violation of the reference high or reference low, whereas a successful break at the TD Magnet Price will often result in an extension to the 1.382 level.

If you apply the same qualifiers as those you use with TD Lines (with a dashed retracement line representing a disqualified level, and a solid line, a qualified level), and if any of the following three conditions is satisfied, then an intrabar upside violation of a TD Relative Retracement level is considered valid, and the likelihood of a close above the TD Relative Retracement level is increased.

■ Three Conditions for Validating a TD Relative Retracement Level: Only One Needs To Be Satisfied for a Qualified Break

Condition One: The close of the price bar one bar before an intrabar upside break of a TD Relative Retracement level must be below the closing price two bars before the intrabar upside break.

Condition Two: If condition one isn't satisfied, then a qualifying break can still occur, if the market opens above a TD Relative Retracement level and then trades one tick above the open.

Condition Three: If the difference between the close of the bar prior to the upside break and its true low (the lesser of that bar's low or the previous close) is calculated, and value of the close of the price bar preceding the upside break is added to that, the result must be less than the TD Relative Retracement level.

If Condition One is satisfied, traders can then initiate long positions at the time of the break, rather than waiting for a bullish confirmation at the close. The rationale is that, if the market closed lower before the upside break, traders did not anticipate an advance and were therefore not positioned for it. They might even have been short—which would have improved the probability of upside follow-through into the close.

The sort of price action of Condition Two suggests that the supply/demand dynamic has shifted in favor of bulls and that renewed buying activity will increase the chances of a close above the upside TD Relative Retracement level.

In the event that neither Condition One nor Two is satisfied, Condition Three, which measures buying pressure ahead of the TD Relative Retracement level, may be applied, to determine whether or not a successful closing break is likely.

The rationale for applying Condition Three to qualify the upside breakout is that buying pressure on the bar of the upside break not only exceeded demand from the previous bar, but also was sufficient to overcome the TD Relative Retracement level.

We now know what conditions need to be fulfilled to qualify an intrabar break, but what should you do if the market fails to follow through to the upside, as originally anticipated? As with TD Lines, DeMark developed a set of contingency criteria that would invalidate an upside break of a TD Relative Retracement level.

▓ Conditions That Invalidate an Upside Break of a TD Relative Retracement Level

Condition One: If the open of the price bar following a qualified upside break is below the TD Relative Retracement level, exit the long position on the open.

Condition Two: If the open of the bar following a qualified upside break is below the close of the breakout bar, and then it closes below the TD Relative Retracement level, exit the long position on the close.

Condition Three: If the high of the bar following the qualified upside break is below the high of the breakout bar, exit the long position on the close.

If any one of the following three conditions is satisfied, then an intrabar downside violation of a TD Relative Retracement level is considered valid, and the likelihood of a close above the TD Relative Retracement level is increased. (See the text below for further explanation.)

▓ Conditions That Qualify a Downside Break of a TD Relative Retracement Level

Condition One: The close of the price bar one bar before an intrabar downside break of a TD Relative Retracement level must be above the closing price two bars before the intrabar downside break.

Condition Two: Assuming condition one isn't satisfied, a qualifying break can still occur if the market opens below a TD Relative Retracement level and then trades one tick below the open.

Condition Three: To measure supply, calculate the difference between the close of the bar prior to the downside break and its true high (the greater of that bar's high or the previous close), and subtract that value from the close of the price bar preceding the downside break. The result must be greater than the TD Relative Retracement level.

Assuming Condition One occurs, traders can initiate short positions at the time of the break, rather than waiting for a bearish confirmation on a closing basis. The rationale for this action is that, if the market closed higher before the downside break, then traders must not have been anticipating a decline and were therefore not positioned for it. They might even have been long—thereby improving the probability of downside follow-through into the close.

The sort of price action of Condition Two suggests the supply/demand dynamic has shifted in favor of bears and that renewed selling activity has increased the chances of a close below the downside TD Relative Retracement level.

In the event that neither Condition One nor Two is satisfied, this third condition, which measures selling pressure ahead of the TD Relative Retracement level, may be applied to determine whether or not a successful closing break is likely.

With Condition Three, the rationale for the downside breakout to be considered valid is that selling pressure on the bar of the downside break not only exceeded supply from the previous bar, but was also sufficient to overcome the TD Relative Retracement level.

■ **To Exit a Short Position After a Qualified Downside Break of a TD Relative Retracement Level**

Condition One: If the open of the price bar following a qualified downside break is above the TD Relative Retracement level, exit your short position on the open.

Condition Two: If the bar following a qualified downside break opens above the close of the breakout bar, and then closes above the TD Relative Retracement level, exit your short position on the close.

Condition Three: If the low of the bar following the qualified downside break is above the low of the breakout bar, exit your short position on the close.

TD Relative Retracement: Recommended Settings

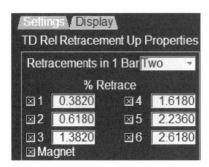
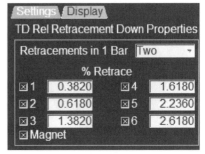

Looking further into retracements, DeMark observed that if the market violates the 0.382 percent upside TD Relative Retracement level intrabar, but closes below it, then one of three scenarios is likely:

More Retracement Scenarios Upside Violations

1. If the close of the breakout bar is below the close of the prior bar, then upside potential is probably exhausted near term.

2. If the close of the breakout bar is higher than the close of the prior bar, then the next key retracement level is half the distance between the 0.382 and 0.618 levels; or

3. If the upside failure happens ahead of the 0.618 level, then the next key retracement level is the midpoint of the 0.618 level and the TD Magnet Price.

If the market violates the 0.382 percent upside TD Relative Retracement level intrabar, but closes above it, then one of two scenarios is likely:

Retracement Scenarios Downside Violations

1. If the breakout bar's close is above the close of the prior bar, then downside potential is probably exhausted near term.

2. If the close of the breakout bar is lower than the prior bar's close, then the next key retracement level is half the distance between the 0.382 and 0.618 levels; or

3. If the downside failure happens ahead of the 0.618 level, then the next key retracement level is the midpoint of the 0.618 level and the TD Magnet Price.

DeMark also mentions that another price pattern should be watched: When a bar exceeds two retracement levels on either the upside or the downside in the same period, the market often reverses course or, at least, consolidates.

Another Reversal/Consolidation Pattern

1. If the market opens below one retracement level and then moves above both it and the retracement level above it; or

2. If the market opens above a retracement level and then trades below both it and the retracement level beyond that, this often coincides with near-term price exhaustion.

TD Relative Retracements are very helpful when you can reference a prior high or low, but what do you do when the market is

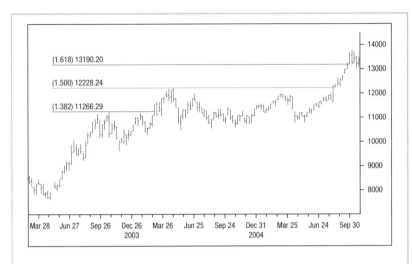

FIGURE 5.3   Upside TD Absolute Retracement

In the weekly chart of the Nikkei 225 (basis cash), note how the market bounces sharply the first time it tests the upside 0.382 TD Absolute Retracement level projected from the February 2003 low. Interestingly, the 0.50 level also provides stiff resistance for the eighteen months after it is first tested.

trading at historic highs or lows and there is no prior reference level? DeMark also has an approach for this situation. He calls it TD Absolute Retracement (**Figures 5.3** and **5.4**).

■ TD Absolute Retracement

To project downside levels, multiply the high by a factor of 0.382 and 0.618, and

To project upside levels, multiply the low by a factor of 0.382 and 0.618.

Recommended Settings for
TD Absolute Retracement

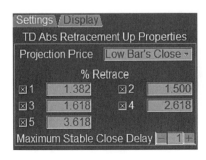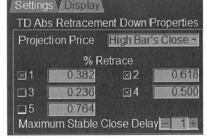

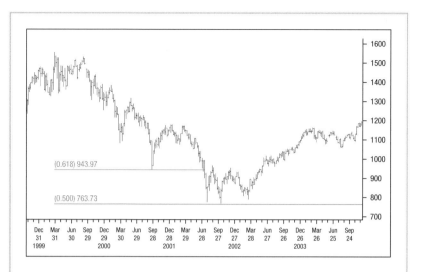

FIGURE 5.4   **Downside TD Absolute Retracement**

In the weekly chart of the S&P 500 (basis cash), note how the market bounces sharply the first time it tests the downside 0.618 TD Absolute Retracement level projected off the March 2000 high. Interestingly, it also bounces sharply in April 2002 off the 0.50 level.

Up until now, we've focused only on retracements of price, but, in doing so, we've overlooked an important factor—retracements of time. DeMark calls his response to this issue *TD Retracement Arc*. Combining price and time adds an extra dimension to the analysis.

Initially, DeMark struggled with the scale issue: Every time a chart was resized, it produced different retracement levels. The solution was to anchor the point of origin used in the construction of the TD Retracement Arc (**Figures 5.5** and **5.6**).

■ Constructing the TD Retracement Arc for Upside Retracements

If you believe the market is basing,

1. Draw a diagonal line originating from your chosen reference low to the highest high traded since the market last traded beneath the reference low;

2. Calculate the 0.382 and 0.618 retracements of the high to the low on that diagonal line; and

3. Project the 0.382 and 0.618 levels forward, using the reference origin as the pivot level.

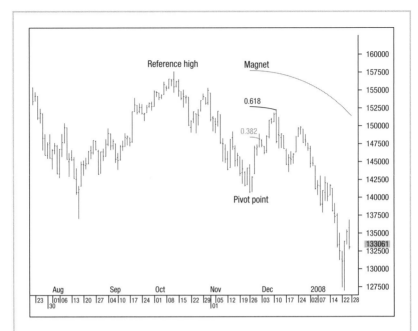

FIGURE 5.5   **Upside TD Retracement Arc**

The daily chart of the S&P 500 (basis cash) illustrates an upside TD Retracement Arc. The arc is constructed after identifying the last time the market traded below the expected reference low and the highest point between those two lows. Using the reference low as the pivot, the 0.382 and 0.618 retracements of that move are projected forward. Note how the 0.618 level coincides with the reversal that occurs on December 11, 2007.

Source: CQG Inc. © 2008. All rights reserved worldwide. www.cqg.com.

▨ Constructing the TD Retracement Arc for Downside Retracements

If you believe the market is topping,

1. Draw a diagonal line originating from your chosen reference high to the lowest low traded since the market last traded above the reference high;

2. Calculate the 0.382 and 0.618 retracements of the low to the high on that diagonal line; and

3. Project the 0.382 and 0.618 levels forward, using the reference origin as the pivot level.

Developing the time aspect a step further shows it to be a useful way to corroborate expected strength or weakness. DeMark notes

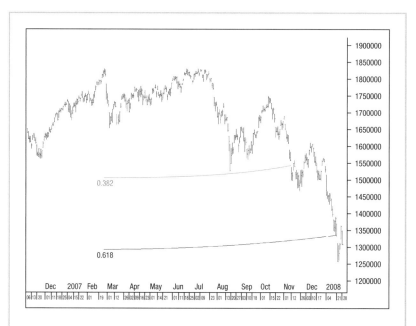

FIGURE 5.6   Downside TD Retracement Arc

The daily chart of the Nikkei 225 (basis cash) illustrates a downside TD Retracement Arc. The arc is constructed after identifying the last time the market traded above the expected reference high and the lowest point between those two highs. Using the reference high as the pivot, the 0.382 and 0.618 retracements of that move are projected forward into the future. Note how the 0.618 level provides strong support in mid-August 2007.

Source: CQG Inc. © 2008. All rights reserved worldwide. www.cqg.com.

that, if, for example, the market can retrace 0.382 of a price move in 0.382 of the amount of time that the original move took to unfold, then there is an increased probability that the market will get to the 0.618 price projection.

As with all the DeMark indicators, you can apply this approach to retracements to any market or time frame, and so it is worth looking at a number of different instruments and time frames, to see if there is a confluence of levels and alignment, such as a 0.382 retracement in a longer-term time frame, with a 0.618 retracement in a shorter-term time frame. Furthermore, you can apply the TD Relative Retracement, TD Absolute Retracement (**Figure 5.7**), and TD Retracement Arc to functions other than price. Consider, for example, applying

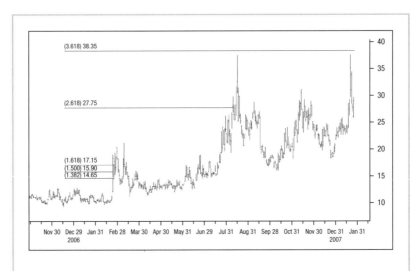

FIGURE 5.7   **An Upside TD Absolute Retracement**

The daily chart of the VIX index illustrates an upside TD Absolute Retracement. Note how the 3.618 level caps the last two sharp moves higher in August 2007 and January 2008.

Source: CQG Inc. © 2008. All rights reserved worldwide. www.cqg.com.

them to implied option volatility, the VIX, or the UBS FX Risk Index (which monitors investor appetite for risk-aversion and risk-seeking behavior).

CHAPTER 6

TD Trend Factor and TD Propulsion

TD Trend Factor

Since I've always been intrigued by price ratios and relationships that try to predict where markets are likely to encounter buying interest or selling interest, DeMark's TD Trend Factor has always held a fascination for me. The indicator isolates qualified highs, lows, and closes, and multiplies those values by a series of predefined ratios in order to identify prospective support and resistance levels. Used in conjunction with other TD studies, TD Trend Factor is a helpful tool for defining potential exhaustion levels or for calculating targets when an expected price reversal is underway.

Many technical analysts ask how DeMark came up with the number sequences and ratios that he uses. More often than not, they were by-products of extensive and obsessive-compulsive experimentation with Fibonacci numbers. The two most commonly used Fibonacci ratios are 0.382 and 0.618. DeMark subtracted the former from the latter, took the 0.236 result, and divided that by four. (It is DeMark's contention that market moves can be subdivided into a series of directional legs and that the inception of a leg is often preceded by a move of approximately 25 percent of the prior leg (see the section "TD Propulsion" for further details).

Although the number 0.236 divided by 4 is 0.059, after rigorous testing in a wide variety of markets, DeMark concluded that 0.0556 was a more accurate and reliable ratio to use for price projections. Additional upside or downside levels are identified by a series of 0.0556 multiples.

What do you do with markets, such as forex (FX), that move in small price increments, which are often quoted to four decimal places?

The solution is to add an extra decimal, so that the upside ratio is 1.00556, while the downside ratio is 0.99444.

Although a factor of 0.0556 is used in upside calculations, the downside projections are derived differently, since each TD Trend Factor level is used to determine the next one (whereby each value is multiplied by 0.9444 for larger values, or 0.99444, for smaller values). We use 5.556 percent as the ratio for upside moves, while 94.44 percent is used as the multiplier for downside moves (compared with 0.5556 percent and 0.9944 percent, respectively, for smaller values).

As is true with all the DeMark indicators, specific sets of rules qualify a high, low, or close from which to project downside or upside TD Trend Factor levels (**Figures 6.1, 6.2**, and **6.3**).

■ To Determine a Top from Which to Calculate

Downside TD Trend Factor Levels

After the market has advanced by at least 5.556 percent from a previous low, compare the close of the high bar with the close of the previous price bar.

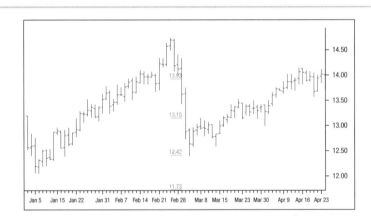

FIGURE 6.1   **Projecting Downside TD Trend Factor Levels**

In the daily chart of silver (basis cash), silver advances by more than 5.556 percent from a prior low, and we can project downside TD Trend Factor levels. Since the close of the high bar from February 26, 2007, is above the close of the prior price bar, the first downside projection is based on the high of the high bar, and all subsequent levels are calculated from the high of the high bar. Note how the market bounces abruptly after it reaches the third downside level on March 5, 2007.

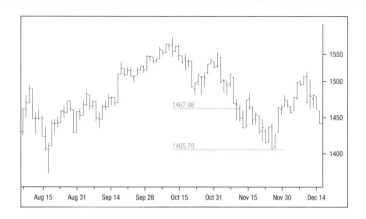

FIGURE 6.2   Projecting Downside TD Trend Factor Levels

In the chart of the S&P 500 (basis cash), the index advances by more than 5.556 percent from a prior low, and we can project downside TD Trend Factor levels. Since the close of the high bar is below the close of the prior price bar, the first downside projection is based on the close of the high bar, and all subsequent levels are calculated from the high of the high bar. Note how the second downside level provides support on November 26, 2007.

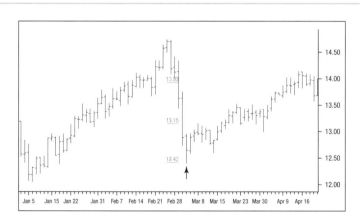

FIGURE 6.3   Projecting Downside Coincident with TD Differential

In the daily chart of silver (basis cash), the failure at the third TD Trend Factor level coincides with a TD Differential buy signal, which indicates upward pressure.

117

If

The close of the high bar is above the close of the previous price bar,

Then

The downside TD Trend Factor projection should be anchored at the high of the high bar.

But if

The close of the high bar close is below the close of previous price bar,

Then

The downside TD Trend Factor projection should be anchored at the close of the high bar.

Note that the first downside TD Trend Factor level (which is taken from either the high or the close of the high bar) projects down by a ratio of 0.9444, but that all subsequent downside TD Trend Factor levels are projected from the peak of the high bar's peak.

■ To Determine a Bottom from Which to Calculate

Upside TD Trend Factor Levels

After the market has declined by at least 5.556 percent from a previous top, compare the close of the low bar with the close of the previous price bar.

If

The close of the low bar is below the close of the previous price bar,

Then

The upside TD Trend Factor projection should be anchored at the low bar's low.

But if

The close of the low bar is above the close of the previous price bar,

Then

The upside TD Trend Factor projection should be anchored at the close of the low bar.

Note that the first upside TD Trend Factor level (which is taken from either the low or the close of the low bar) projects up by a multiple of 1.0556, but all subsequent upside TD Trend Factor levels (**Figures 6.4, 6.5,** and **6.6**) are projected from the trough of the low bar.

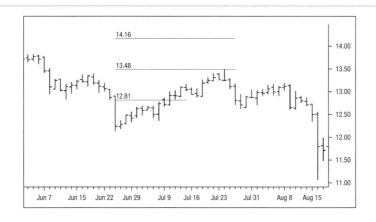

FIGURE 6.4   **Projecting Upside TD Trend Factor Levels**

The daily chart shows that silver declines by more than 5.556 percent from a prior high, and we can project upside TD Trend Factor levels. Since the close of the low bar is below the close of the prior price bar, the first upside projection is based on the low of the low bar, and all subsequent levels are calculated from the low of the low bar. Note how the market sells off sharply after hitting the second TD Trend Factor level.

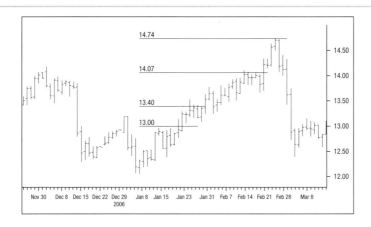

FIGURE 6.5   **Projecting Upside TD Trend Factor Levels**

In the daily chart, silver (basis cash) declines by more than 5.556 percent from a prior high, and we can project upside TD Trend Factor levels. In this instance, since the close of the low bar on January 8 is above the close of the prior price bar, the first upside projection is based on the close of the low bar, and all subsequent levels are calculated from the low of the low bar. Note how the fourth upside projection rebuffs the advance on February 26, 2007.

119

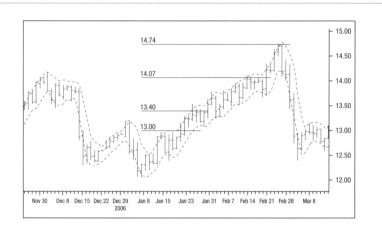

FIGURE 6.6   Projecting Upside TD Trend Factor Levels

In the daily chart of silver (basis cash), the failure at the fourth TD Trend Factor level coincides with two consecutive closes outside TD Channel II (see Chapter 9), which indicates downside vulnerability.

Frequently Asked Questions

Is there a set of conditions I can use to qualify TD Trend Factor violations?

Yes, you can use the same three criteria that define a qualified/disqualified TD Line or TD Retracement break.

Can I use TD Trend Factor in conjunction with other TD indicators?

Yes, you can, and you should. If you have a confluence of signals, using TD indicators together is invariably more powerful and has a greater probability of working—particularly if it coincides with a TD Channel, TD Sequential, TD Combo, or TD D-Wave signal, or if the TD Trend Factor level lines up with a TD Retracement and/or a TD Propulsion level.

Are there any other interesting things I could experiment with, with the DeMark indicators?

Yes, you can try to apply TD Trend Factor to TD Setup ranges.

TD Trend Factor – Recommended Settings

Settings / Display		
TD Trend Factor Up Properties		
Levels to Display		
Full Levels		Half Levels
☒1 ☒3 ☒5		☐1 ☐3
☒2 ☒4		☐2 ☐4
Maximum Stable Close Delay	− 2 +	

Settings / Display		
TD Trend Factor Down Properties		
Levels to Display		
Full Levels		Half Levels
☒1 ☒3 ☒5		☐1 ☐3
☒2 ☒4		☐2 ☐4
Maximum Stable Close Delay	− 2 +	

TD Propulsion

TD Propulsion has a number of useful facets, which make it an interesting indicator. In addition to identifying prospective price-exhaustion levels, it also highlights trends in progress. It operates on the premise that, if a market rallies, pulls back, and then resumes its uptrend without having violated the origin of the advance, you can identify a bull trigger that should provide the catalyst for an extension to a higher target level.

Conversely, if a market declines, rallies, and then resumes its downtrend without having violated the origin of the decline, you can identify a bear trigger that should provide the catalyst for an extension to a lower target level.

The indicator has two components: primary levels, referred to as *TD Propulsion Up* and *TD Propulsion Down* entry points, and secondary levels, known as *TD Propulsion Up Target* and *TD Propulsion Down Target*. The primary (thrust) levels serve as triggers for extended moves in the direction of the trend toward the secondary (exhaustion) levels.

Defining the initial thrust level properly is crucial to the construction of TD Propulsion. To do that properly, you need to consider price action leading up to and subsequent to the primary advance. Both the price decline leading up to a prospective primary upthrust and the subsequent setback need to be taken into consideration— and these moves are validated if they satisfy a minimum percentage requirement.

■ **Defining the Initial Thrust Level for an Advance**

Calculate the difference in price between the price low of the move up at point X and the price high for the move so far at point Y.

If

The sell-off from the closes of the high bars leading up to points X and Z are 23.6 percent or more of the difference between X and Y,

Then

1. Points X and Z are correctly identified;

2. The initial upthrust from Z to A is 23.6 percent of the rally from X to Y, that value is added to the low at Z, and

3. The upside price target for B is double the percentage (2 × 23.6 percent), or 47.2 percent.

■ **Defining the Initial Thrust Level for a Decline**

Calculate the difference in price between the price high of the move down at point X and the price low for the move so far at point Y.

If

The advance from the closes of the low bars leading up to points X and Z are 23.6 percent or more of the difference between X and Y,

Then

1. Points X and Z are correctly identified,

2. The initial downthrust from Z to A is 23.6 percent of the decline from X to Y, that value is subtracted from the high at Z, and

3. The downside price target for B is double the percentage (2 × 23.6 percent), or 47.2 percent.

Note that, on the Bloomberg terminal, the default settings for TD Propulsion are set to the more conservative 25 percent and 50 percent thresholds, rather than 23.6 percent and 47.2 percent, respectively.

More conservative traders may wish to apply one of the three TD Line qualification criteria to determine whether the market, figuratively speaking, is anticipating a breakout. If one of the qualifiers is satisfied prior to clearing a TD Propulsion Up or a TD Propulsion Down level, then the probability of follow-through in the direction of the break is increased (**Figures 6.7** and **6.8**).

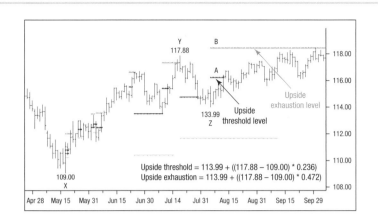

FIGURE 6.7   **The TD Propulsion Up Level**

In the daily chart of USDJPY, calculate the difference in price between the price low at point X and the price high at point Y. As long as the sell-offs from the closes of the high bars leading up to points X and Z are 23.6 percent or more of the difference between X and Y, then points X and Z are correctly identified. The ensuing up move off Z encounters resistance at A, the TD Propulsion Up level (upside threshold level). Once the market overcomes that level, the thrust provides the catalyst for an extension to B (upside exhaustion level). The initial advance from Z to A is 23.6 percent of the rally from X to Y, and that value is added to the low at Z, while B is double the percentage (23.6) at 47.2 percent.

TD Propulsion: Recommended Settings

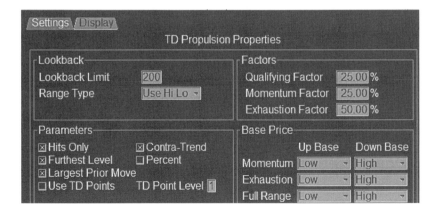

	Color	Size	Display
Settings \ Display			
TD Propulsion Properties			
Up Momentum	Green	1	☒
Up Exhaustion	Cyan	1	☒
Up Full Range	Blue	1	☐
Down Momentum	Yellow	1	☒
Down Exhaustion	Red	1	☒
Down Full Range	Light Red	1	☐
Up Origin	Magenta		☐
Down Origin	Red		☐

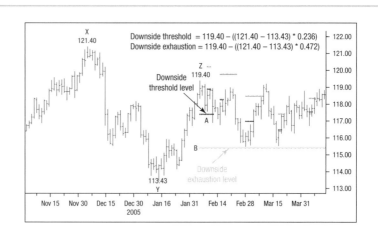

FIGURE 6.8

In the daily chart of USDJPY, calculate the difference in price between the price high at point X and the price low at point Y. As long as the advance from the closes of the low bars to points X and Z are 23.6 percent or more of the difference between X and Y, then points X and Z are correctly identified. The ensuing down move from point Z encounters support at the TD Propulsion Down level (downside threshold). Once the market violates that level, the thrust provides the catalyst for an extension to the downside exhaustion level. The initial decline from Z to A is 23.6 percent of the decline from X to Y, subtracted from the high at Z, while B is double that value at 47.2 percent.

CHAPTER 7

TD Oscillators

TD Range Expansion Index (TD REI)

It never ceases to amaze me how many people use technical indicators without knowing the formulas for the studies. If you don't believe me, take a quick pop quiz: See if you can write down the calculation for the Relative Strength Index (RSI), one of the most commonly used overbought/oversold momentum oscillators.

Not as easy as you thought, right?

■ *In Case You Need Prompting on the RSI . . .*

Take the last fourteen price bars and compare the strength of up and down moves over that period. By averaging the up and down moves between bars on a closing basis, you get Relative Strength (RS).

To convert RS to index format (RSI) . . .

RSI = 100[100/1 + RS].

Okay, so your memory's failing—you used to know the formula years ago. Does it really matter that you've forgotten it, now that you're a seasoned trader and you've been using it for years?

Well, yes, it does, because, if you don't know how the indicator is constructed, it is unlikely that you will know its shortcomings and when it is more or less likely to work effectively, under different market conditions.

Many of the momentum-based indicators included on charting systems these days are derived exponentially rather than arithmetically. Accordingly, large price movements have a tendency to distort historical data and studies based on that price action (albeit less significantly as more time elapses). Furthermore, because most chart-based technical indicators are derived from closing prices, the relevance of intrabar trading activity between highs and lows is often overlooked.

Many people concentrate—too heavily in my opinion—on the notion of "divergence" between price action and momentum, to identify prospective turning points in the established trend. Divergence manifests itself when an extreme price high or low is not matched by a corresponding extreme in momentum. When *bearish* divergence occurs during an uptrend, for example, conventional wisdom argues that positive momentum, that is, the ability to maintain intrabar gains on a closing basis, must be on the wane, since upside pressure is dissipating.

Conversely, *bullish* divergence between price action and momentum is thought to exist when intrabar losses are not sustained on a closing basis, implying that downward pressure on prices is receding.

DeMark takes issue with this interpretation of momentum, arguing that momentum divergences don't happen often, but, when they do, it's fairly common for multiple divergences to occur. This makes it difficult to discern when threatening divergence between price action and momentum will trigger a reversal in price. (For example, take a look at the daily chart of gold, below (**Figure 7.1**), which has a fairly pronounced divergence between price and the fourteen-period RSI for a prolonged period of time, even though the market remained firmly entrenched in an uptrend.)

DeMark notes that, in addition to monitoring price, we should pay attention to the amount of time that momentum indicators spend in overbought/oversold territory—a concept he calls *duration analysis*. He observes that a reading of six or fewer price bars, in either overbought or oversold territory, is mild, irrespective of how extreme that reading happens to be. An excursion of more than six price bars into overbought or oversold territory, however, suggests that a trend is strong.

Refuting the widely held notion that markets are most susceptible to reversals when in extreme overbought/oversold territory, he

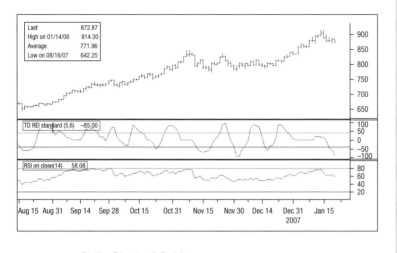

FIGURE 7.1 **Daily Chart of Gold**

Note how pronounced bearish divergence between price action and momentum was throughout the up-move between September and October.

further argues that reversals are most likely to occur from mildly overbought/oversold levels. Ideally, extreme momentum readings need to revert to neutral levels, and then correct back toward mildly overbought or oversold territory, before a meaningful reversal can begin. It's this interplay between extreme and mild momentum readings that produces failure swings and leads people to believe in divergence.

It's all very well being a back-seat, momentum driver, you say, but what does DeMark have to say about momentum? He notes that, although there are numerous factors influencing the market on a day-to-day basis, the effects of those factors subside over time, and he developed the TD Range Expansion Index (TD REI), for just such situations (**Figure 7.2**). It is silent throughout strong directional moves and neutral during trading ranges; it is, in other words, responsive to advances and declines in price.

The effects of sudden price bursts that are not sustained for more than one price bar can be mitigated by evaluating the relationship between the current price bar and the price bar two bars before it.

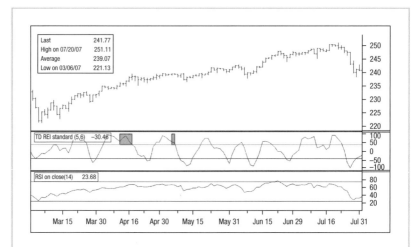

FIGURE 7.2   **TD REI Price Fluctuations**

Note how in the daily chart of GBPJPY the TD REI is much more responsive to price fluctuations than the RSI is. While the RSI remains overbought during the uptrend from February through May 2007 and again from June through July, the TD REI provides a buying opportunity in late March, mid-May, mid-June, and late June.

■ TD REI Formula

Calculation:

1. Add the difference between the high of the current price bar and the high two bars earlier to the difference between the low of the current price bar and the low two bars earlier. *(The result can be either above or below zero, depending on whether the current high and low are greater than, or less than, the high or low two price bars earlier and, if so, by how much.)*

Analysis:

Current price action is overlapping earlier price action, and the markets are *not* exhibiting strong directional tendencies if the following occurs:

1. The high of the current price bar is greater than, or equal to, the low five or six bars earlier, or the high of two bars ago is greater than, or equal to, the close seven or eight bars earlier; *and*

2. The low of the current price bar is less than, or equal to, the high five or six bars earlier, or the high of two bars ago is less than, or equal to, the close seven or eight bars earlier.

If either one of the two qualifiers is not satisfied, however, the corresponding bar is assigned a value of zero, instead of the value that would otherwise have been assigned. The rationale is that, if these conditions aren't met, the market is probably trending, because the current price isn't overlapping earlier price action. The zero value, therefore, reduces the risk that the indicator will become overbought or oversold during a directional move, and thus prevents traders from calling a top or bottom prematurely during a strong trend.

▥ To Establish a Value for the TD REI

1. Add the difference between the high and low for each bar of a five-bar period,

2. Total all the values,

3. Divide the result by the absolute price move over the five-bar period (that is, the difference between the highest high and lowest low), and

4. Multiply that result by one hundred to determine the TD REI (which can trade between −100 and +100).

For identifying prospective reversals relative to overbought and oversold zones for the TD REI, DeMark considers +40 and −40 to be the ideal parameters. When the TD REI is above +40 for fewer than six price bars, and then falls back, that's a sign of weakness, and you should expect some near-term gains. When it's below −40 for fewer than six price bars, and then recovers, that's a sign of strength, and you should be prepared for a short-term recovery.

▥ Using the TD REI to Identify Prospective Reversals

Weakness: TD REI stays above +40 for fewer than six price bars, and then falls back. *(Expect near-term gains.)*

Strength: TD REI stays below −40 for fewer than six price bars, and then recovers. *(Expect short-term recovery.)*

You can add a further filter, the TD Price Oscillator Qualifier (TD POQ), as a means of filtering the signals generated by the TD REI. (Incidentally, you can also apply this filter to other overbought/oversold momentum-based oscillators.)

■ Using the TD POQ to Filter TD REI Signals Further

To Initiate a Buy Signal:

1. The TD REI must be below −40 for six or fewer periods;

2. There must be a lower close than the close of the prior price bar;

3. The open of the next price bar must be less than, or equal to, the two prior price highs; and

4. The market must trade above the open and post a high above either one of the prior two price highs.

To Trigger a Sell Signal:

1. The TD REI must be above +40 for six or fewer periods;

2. There must be a higher close than the close of the prior price bar;

3. The open of the next price bar must be greater than, or equal to, the two prior price lows; and

4. The market must trade below the open and post a low below either one of the prior two price lows.

Also notice that, when the TD REI is overbought for more than six price bars and then goes into oversold territory for fewer than six price bars, it often provides an acute risk/reward buying opportunity.

Conversely, when the TD REI is oversold for more than six price bars and then goes into overbought territory for fewer than six price bars, it often provides an acute risk/reward selling opportunity, when it exits overbought territory within six bars (**Figures 7.3** and **7.4**).

■ For the Mathematicians

Legend:

H = Current price bar's high

H_2 = The high two bars ago

L = Current price bar's low

L_2 = The low two bars ago

$X = (H - H_2) + (L - L_2)$

Condition I: The high of the current price bar must be greater than or equal to the low five or six bars earlier,

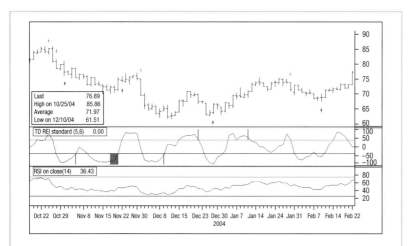

FIGURE 7.3   **TD REI Responsive to Price Fluctuations**

Note how in the daily chart of crude oil (WTI) the TD REI is much more responsive to price fluctuations than the RSI when prices are trending. While there are no clear signals from the RSI between October and February, the TD REI provides a number of directional opportunities throughout that time.

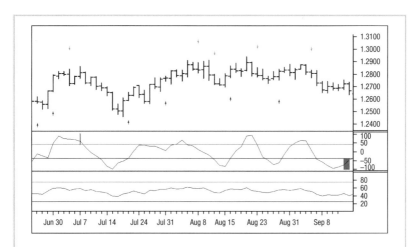

FIGURE 7.4   **TD REI Responsive to Price Fluctuations**

In the daily chart of EURUSD, the TD REI is much more responsive to price fluctuations than the RSI, even when prices are confined to ranges. While there are no clear signals from the RSI between June and September, the TD REI provides a number of directional opportunities throughout that time.

Or

The high of two bars ago must be greater than or equal to the close seven or eight bars earlier, *and*

Condition II: The low of the current price bar must be less than, or equal to, the high either five or six bars earlier,

Or

The high of two bars ago must be less than or equal to the close either seven or eight bars earlier.

If either condition is not satisfied, a value of zero is assigned to that bar.

If both conditions are met, the value for that bar is the difference between the high and low.

$$Y = (\text{Sum } X_1 \ldots X_5)$$
$$H_5 = \text{the highest high over the last five bars}$$
$$L_5 = \text{the lowest low over the last five bars}$$
$$\text{TD REI} = (Y / (H_5 - L_5)) \times 100$$

TD REI: Recommended Settings

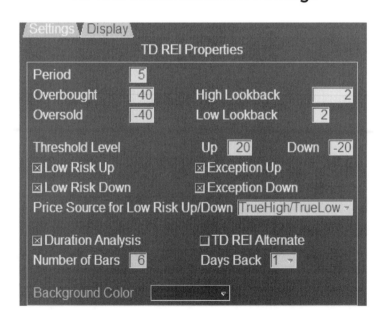

TD Demarker I and TD Demarker II

TD DeMarker I. TD DeMarker I is similar to TD REI, in that it attempts to differentiate between trending and nontrending markets, and then, having defined the underlying directional bias, it looks for short-term reversals based on how the indicator responds to over-bought and oversold levels. Specifically, TD DeMarker I takes the high and low of the current price bar and compares them with the corresponding high and low of the previous price bar. If the current high is greater than, or equal to, the previous high, the difference is calculated and the resulting value stored.

▪ TD DeMarker I

To Arrive at the Numerator:

1. If the current high is below the prior high, the bar is assigned a value of zero, and the values added to one another over a period of thirteen price bars.
2. The low of the current price bar is then compared with the low of the prior bar, and, if the current low is less than, or equal to, the previous price bar's low, the difference between the two is stored.
3. If the low of the current price bar is above the prior low, the bar is assigned a value of zero, and the values over a period of thirteen price bars added to one another, and to the result of the calculation of the relationships between the highs.

To Arrive at the Denominator:

Add the numerator to the sum of the result from the low price comparisons to arrive at the denominator.

To Arrive at the TD DeMarker I:

Divide the numerator by the denominator.

The result will fluctuate between zero and one hundred, with overbought and over-sold zones set at 60 and 40, respectively.

As with the TD REI, the amount of time that TD DeMarker I spends in either overbought or oversold territory (its duration) helps to distinguish between ranges and mild and strong trends (**Figure 7.5**). That said, it is not enough for the indicator simply to be overbought or oversold; for a prospective buy, other conditions should also be satisfied.

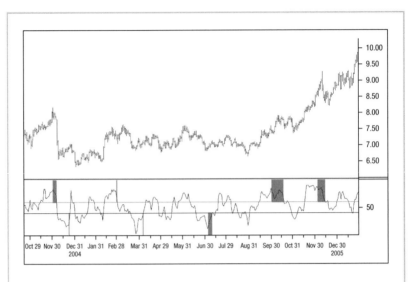

FIGURE 7.5   **Overbought Territory**

In the daily chart of silver (basis spot), the shaded areas on TD DeMarker I represent times when the market is in extreme overbought or oversold territory. If the indicator is in extreme overbought territory for more than thirteen periods and then subsequently goes mildly overbought before returning to neutral, this often coincides with an interim top. If prices are in extreme overbought territory, and then TD DeMarker I goes below 50 before becoming mildly overbought, it often signals a resumption of the uptrend. (The reverse is true for extreme oversold readings.)

■ Other Conditions That Must Be Satisfied for a Prospective Buy

1. There must be an indicator reading below 40 for thirteen bars or fewer,

2. The close must be less than the low either one or two price bars earlier,

3. The close must be below the prior close and the open,

4. The open of the following bar should be less than, or equal to, the closes of either of the previous two bars, and

5. The price must trade above one of the prior closes.

As soon as this sequence of events occurs, there is an opportunity for a long entry. For a prospective sell, there are also conditions that must be satisfied.

■ Other Conditions That Must Be Satisfied for a Prospective Sell

1. There must be an indicator reading above 60 for six bars or fewer,

2. The close must be greater than the high either one or two price bars earlier,

3. The close must be above the prior close and the open,

4. The open of the following bar should be above, or equal to, the closes of either of the previous two bars, and

5. The price must trade below one of the prior closes.

As soon as this sequence of events occurs, an opportunity exists for a short entry.

TD DeMarker I: Recommended Settings

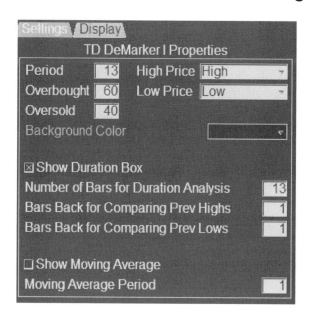

TD DeMarker II. Unlike TD REI and TD DeMarker I, which compare current highs and lows with highs and lows one bar earlier, TD DeMarker II looks at a number of price relationships to measure buying and selling pressure (**Figure 7.6**).

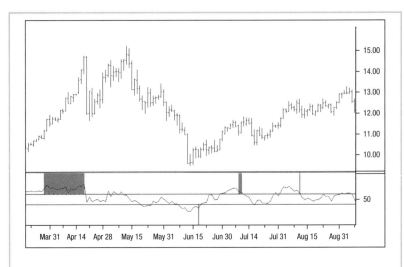

FIGURE 7.6   **Overbought Territory**

In the daily chart of silver (basis spot), the shaded areas on TD DeMarker II represent times when the market is in extreme overbought or oversold territory. If the indicator is in extreme overbought territory for more than eight periods and then subsequently goes mildly overbought before returning to neutral, this often coincides with an interim top. If prices are in extreme overbought territory and then TD DeMarker II goes below 50 before becoming mildly overbought, it often signals a resumption of the uptrend. (The reverse is true for extreme oversold readings.)

■ TD DeMarker II

(To Measure Buying Pressure)

To Arrive at the Numerator:

1. Look at the difference between the high of the current price bar and the close of the previous bar's close, over a period of eight bars,

2. Add the result to the difference between the close of the current bar and its true low over a period of eight bars,

3. Subtract the previous close from the current high, and

4. Assign any negative returns a value of zero.

To Arrive at the Denominator:

Add

1. The numerator,

2. The difference between the low of the current price bar and the close of the previous bar in the same eight-bar period, and

3. The difference between the current bar's true high and its close.

Note: This difference is referred to as the selling-pressure value.

TD DeMarker II: Recommended Settings

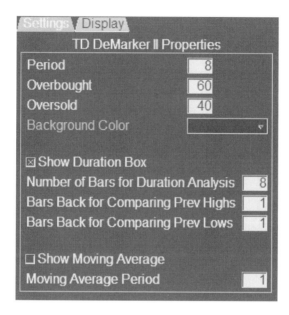

TD Pressure

DeMark believes that price action is directly influenced by supply and demand factors. Since a change in volume often precedes price moves, it makes sense to combine indicators that measure the rate of change in price with indicators that measure the rate of volume change. TD Pressure does this, while incorporating a rate of change in accumulation and distribution of this data (**Figure 7.7**).

The starting point for the accumulation/distribution measurement is the indicator On Balance Volume (OBV):

■ The OBV Indicator

The OBV indicator generates a cumulative volume-based index derived from the relationship between the current and previous day's close.

For example:

If the current day's close is above the previous day's close, the current day's volume is added to the index.

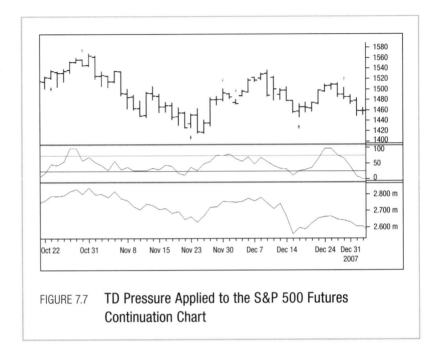

FIGURE 7.7   **TD Pressure Applied to the S&P 500 Futures Continuation Chart**

If the current day's close is below the previous day's close, volume is deducted from the index.

DeMark argues, however, that the relationship between the current day's open and its close is far more important, and a better representation of demand and supply, than the comparison between the current day's close and the previous day's close. Substituting the current day's open for the previous day's close is an improvement, but it is still somewhat misleading.

It is for this reason that DeMark devised a ratio by subtracting the current day's open from the current day's close, divided by the current day's range, which assigns percentages to buying and selling pressure. That ratio is multiplied by the current day's volume numbers, and the result is totaled over time. This makes much more sense, since, if the market closes above its open, and the open happened also to be the day's low, it is a reasonable assumption that 100 percent of all price action that day was buying pressure.

Conversely, if the market closes below the open, and the open that day happens to coincide with the high, it is fair to conclude that 100 percent of all price action was selling pressure. The results are aggregated over time in such a way that buying pressure is divided by the absolute value of buying plus selling pressure, to determine a percentage that can be plotted as an overbought/oversold indicator. Arrows appear when the index moves out of overbought or oversold territory.

Note: Futures markets incorporate open interest (whereas stocks don't), and, so, dividing volume by open interest, and then multiplying that ratio by volume, is a clearer representation of buying and selling pressure.

DeMark uses a five-price-bar period and compares the current close and open, divided by the current day's range, and multiplied by the current day's volume. The five-bar ratio of that buying pressure is totaled and then divided by the absolute value of those five price bars.

TD Pressure: Recommended Settings

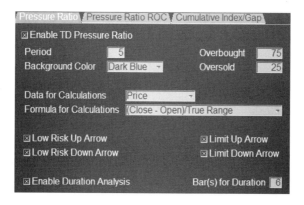

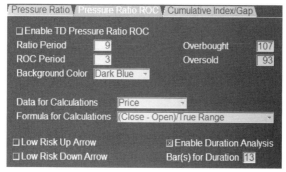

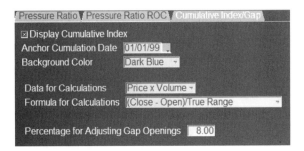

TD Rate of Change (TD ROC)

TD ROC is an integral component of TD Alignment, but can also be used in isolation as an overbought/oversold indicator (**Figure 7.8**).

■ To Determine the TD ROC

Divide the close of the current price bar by the close twelve price bars earlier.

Note: The associated overbought/oversold band fluctuates between 97.5 percent and 102.50 percent (the market is considered neutral when trading stays between these levels).

As with other TD oscillators, the amount of time spent in overbought/ oversold territory is critical for differentiating between mild and extreme readings. Mild overbought/oversold readings often coincide with near-term reversals, while extreme overbought/oversold readings are indicative of strong buying/selling pressure. When mild readings are observed, opportunistic short-term buying and selling opportunities exist. To generate a trading opportunity when extreme readings are seen, look for a return to neutral territory, followed by a mild reading.

TD ROC: Recommended Settings

TD Rate of Change Properties			
Periods	12		
Overbought	102.50	Oversold	97.50
Duration	15	Duration Type	Both
Source	Close	Background Color	Dark Blue

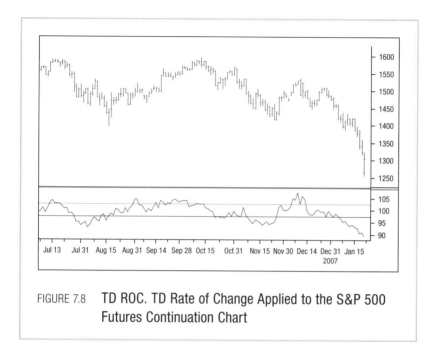

FIGURE 7.8 **TD ROC. TD Rate of Change Applied to the S&P 500 Futures Continuation Chart**

TD Alignment

TD Alignment (**Figure 7.9**) is a composite indicator that combines the following five TD oscillators to measure buying and selling pressure: TD DeMarker I, TD DeMarker II, TD Pressure, TD Range Expansion Index, and TD Rate of Change. Each of the indicators has its own distinct method of measuring overbought/oversold conditions.

■ **TD Alignment**

Combine:

TD DeMarker I,

TD DeMarker II,

TD Pressure,

TD Range Expansion Index, and

TD Rate of Change.

When the indicator is *above* the predefined overbought zone, it is given a value of +1, and,

When the indicator is *below* the predefined oversold zone, it is assigned a value of −1.

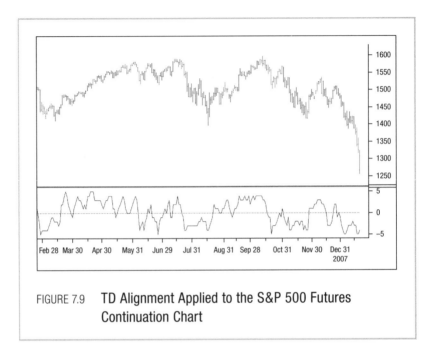

FIGURE 7.9   TD Alignment Applied to the S&P 500 Futures
Continuation Chart

■ **To Produce the Composite TD Alignment Indicator,**
Aggregate the values so they fluctuate between −5 and +5.

Extreme TD Alignment readings at either −5 or +5 are often
associated with near-term price exhaustion, particularly when combined with other TD indicators like TD Sequential or TD Combo.
*Note: The recommended settings for the components of TD Alignment differ
from the recommended defaults for those constituent indicators when they are
used independently.*

TD Alignment: Recommended Settings:

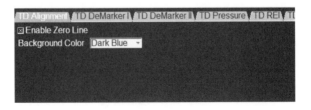

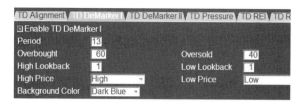

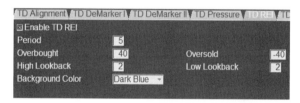

CHAPTER 8

TD Moving Averages

MOVING AVERAGES are perhaps the most widely used market analysis tools, applied by technical and fundamental traders alike. In my experience, however, the trend is like a parachute: If it's not there for you the first time you really need it to work, then it's unlikely you'll ever have much use for it again. As anyone who has traded the currency markets in recent years will tell you, moving averages are all well and good when prices are trending smoothly, but they have a number of shortcomings.

First, they tend to get whipsawed when prices are trading laterally for prolonged periods of time, and second, moving averages lag price action, and so the entry and exit signals they generate are inherently inefficient. Of course, you can increase the length of the moving average to reduce the whipsaw risk, but that simply means that the indicator becomes less responsive to fluctuations in price, and therefore less effective at identifying changes in the trend during the early stages of a reversal. Tom DeMark developed TD Moving Average I and TD Moving Average II to address these concerns.

TD Moving Average I was originally intended to be used as a trailing stop-loss as a means of exiting an established position, but, over time, it has proved particularly useful in determining if a market is trending, and, if so, in providing entry points to initiate a trade in line with the expected directional move. As with all the TD indicators, this study is based on relative price action, and so you can apply it to any market or time frame without having to change any of the default settings. So it's worth keeping an eye on multiple time frames and monitoring them when there is a confluence of bullish, bearish, or neutral signals.

■ To Identify a Prospective Bullish Trend

If

There is a price low that is higher than all twelve prior price lows,

Then

It's likely that selling pressure is waning and the market is predisposed to advancing, near term.

TD Moving Average I serves to recognize this newly positive development.

■ Plotting a Bullish TD Moving Average I

TD Moving Average I plots a five-bar moving average of the lows and extends it for another four price bars, that is, the current price bar and three more into the future.

If, within the next four price bars,

The market fails to post a fresh low above all twelve prior lows,

Then

The moving average of the lows disappears.

But if, within the four-bar extension period,

The market *does* record a low greater than all twelve previous lows,

Then

The five-bar moving average of the lows will continue for another four bars.

This way, the moving average of the lows (**Figure 8.1**) remains in place as long as the market continues to exhibit signs of strength. You should use TD Moving Average I in conjunction with other DeMark indicators, but, if you are already in a long position, you should remain so, unless the market closes beneath the five-bar moving average of the lows and then the next bar opens below it.

■ To Identify a Prospective Bearish Trend

If

There is a price high that is lower than all twelve prior price highs,

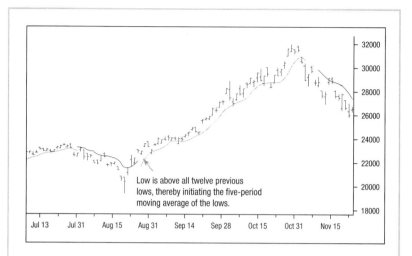

FIGURE 8.1   **TD Moving Average I**

In the daily chart of the Hang Seng, the five-period moving average of the lows is initiated when the market records a low that is above all twelve prior lows. The average is extended for a further four price bars into the future every time the condition is satisfied. You would remain bullish unless the market closes below the average and then opens below it the following bar.

Then

It is likely that buying interest has abated and the market is predisposed to selling off near term.

TD Moving Average I recognizes this newly negative development.

■ Plotting a Bearish TD Moving Average I

TD Moving Average I plots a five-bar moving average of the highs and extends it for another four price bars, that is, for the current price bar and three more into the future.

If, within the next four price bars,

The market fails to post a fresh high below all twelve prior highs,

Then

The moving average of the highs disappears.

But *if*

The market does record a high lower than all twelve previous highs within the four-bar extension period,

Then

The five-bar moving average of the highs will continue for another four price bars.

This way, the moving average of the highs (**Figure 8.2**) remains in place as long as the market continues to show signs of weakness. You should use TD Moving Average I in conjunction with other DeMark indicators, but, if you're already bearish and the market is trading beneath the five-bar moving average of the highs, you should remain short, unless the market closes above the average and then opens above it at the next bar.

In addition to providing an insight into when to close out a trade, TD Moving Average I is helpful in a number of other ways, such as, when a moving average of either the lows or the highs is plotted,

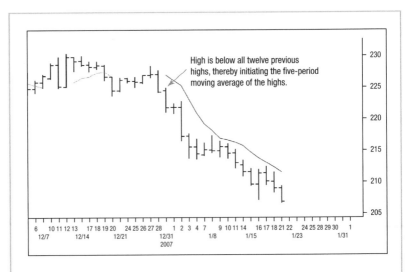

High is below all twelve previous highs, thereby initiating the five-period moving average of the highs.

FIGURE 8.2   **TD Moving Average I**

In the daily chart of GBPJPY, the five-period moving average of the highs is initiated when the market records a high that is below all twelve prior highs. The average is extended for a further four price bars into the future every time the condition is satisfied. You would remain bearish unless the market closes above the average and then opens beyond it the following bar.

when it indicates that the market has momentum behind it and can be traded directionally. As such, it provides a good level from which to initiate either long positions, following dips to the moving average of the lows, or short positions, following rallies to the moving average of the highs.

Conversely, when no moving average is being plotted, no discernable trend exists, and traders should not be initiating directional trades at that time.

TD Moving Average I: Recommended Settings

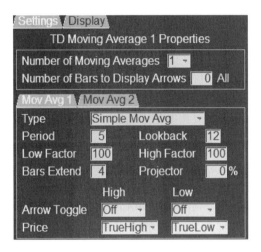

For die-hard trend followers, DeMark offers an alternative, TD Moving Average II, which remains true to the cause in the sense that it consists of two conventional simple moving averages—one short term and one long term, based on closing prices. In this instance, those lengths are three bars and thirty-four bars, respectively. Unlike traditional moving averages, however, TD Moving Average II applies a rate of change (ROC), to each of the averages. The color of the moving averages changes when the ROC switches to positive (blue), or to negative (red).

Whereas TD Moving Average I needs a specific condition to be met in order to appear on the chart (so it can indicate the market is trending), TD Moving Average II (**Figure 8.3**) is always displayed. As is the case with regular moving averages, the relative position of

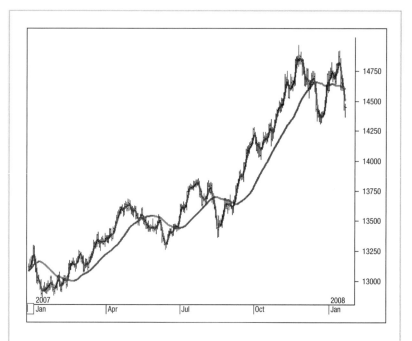

FIGURE 8.3   TD Moving Average II

In this chart, TD Moving Average II is applied to a daily chart of EURUSD. Note how there tends to be more follow-through when rates of change in both averages move in the same direction. The follow-through improves the quality of the signals during periods of consolidation, while still showing responsiveness to breakouts.

Source: CQG, Inc. © 2008 All rights reserved worldwide. www.cqg.com.

the two periods determines the overall trend; that is, when the three-period moving average is above the thirty-four–period moving average, the general tone is considered positive.

Conversely, when the three-period moving average is below the thirty-four–period moving average, the general tone is thought to be negative, but, in this current form, you're still exposed to whipsaw risk. So TD Moving Average II takes things to another level by adding a ROC. Both the short-term and the longer-term averages are compared to their values a predefined number of bars earlier. The current value of the three-period moving average is compared to the corresponding value two price bars earlier, while the thirty-four-period moving average is compared with its value one bar before.

Trading with moving averages still has its shortcomings, and signals indicating a reversal in trend will always lag price action to an extent, but combining the two averages, evaluating where they are in relation to each other, and then overlaying a rate of change, should at the very least, over time, reduce the extent to which you get whip-sawed when markets are not trending.

CHAPTER 9

TD Range Projection, TD Range Expansion Breakout, and TD Channels

TD Range Projection

EXPERIENCE IS THE BEST TEACHER. The future always seems so much clearer in hindsight—which is why we can all relate to the thought "If I'd known then what I know now. . . ." I suppose that's why I'm so intrigued by the market-timing studies developed by Tom DeMark, many of which are forward-looking in the sense that they anticipate prices, an important distinction from other studies. Take TD Range Projection, for example, the indicator that compares the current close with the same price bar's opening, high, and low, to forecast a high/low range for the following price bar. Comparing the current close with the prior close can be somewhat misleading—particularly for stocks, where news is often announced after market close or before market open. The market's closing higher the current day than it did the previous day suggests buying interest, but could lead to missing a situation in which the current day's close is below the previous day's open, which is actually a sign of weakness. Consequently, DeMark considers the relationship between the current bar's open and close to be more significant than the comparison of the current close to the previous bar's close.

This study can be applied to any market or time frame, from ticks to years, but DeMark's preference, and my own as well, is to use it for daily price bars. If you're relating the current close of a specified time period with the corresponding open, one of three possible scenarios is likely:

1. That the current day's closing price is above the current day's opening price, or

2. That the current day's closing price is below the current day's opening price, or

3. That the current day's closing price is equal to the current day's opening price.

■ The Three Possible Scenarios and How to Calculate Them

1. *If* the current day's closing price is above the current day's opening price,

Then X = ((2 + current day's high + current day's low + current day's close) / 2).

2. *If* the current day's closing price is below the current day's opening price,

Then X = ((current day's high + 2 × current day's low + current day's close) / 2).

3. *If* the current day's closing price is equal to the current day's opening price,

Then X = ((current day's high + current day's low + 2 × current day's close) / 2).

To calculate the expected low for the following day,

Subtract the current day's high from X.

To derive the following day's projected high,

Subtract the current day's low from X.

More often than not, the following day's open will be somewhere in between the projected high and low (see **Figure 9.1**); in which case, there's a reasonable chance that the projected range will contain price action for the day. If accompanied by other intraday TD buy or sell signals, these situations would provide acute risk/reward opportunities to buy dips toward the lower end of the day's range forecast, and to sell rallies toward the top end of the day's anticipated range. Nevertheless, we shouldn't write everything off when the following day opens either below the expected low or above the expected high. Such an occurrence tells us that the supply/demand dynamics have shifted, and that in itself is useful information. When the market opens above the projected high or below the projected low, it is often a reflection of the near-term trend as price action continues in the direction of the breakout for the remainder of the day.

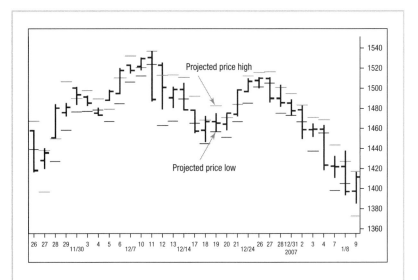

FIGURE 9.1   **TD Range Projection: Projecting Highs and Lows**

In the daily chart of the March 2008 S&P 500 futures, note how the projected high and low provide a useful guide to the day's trading activity.

We can glean even more insight into the following price bar's expected activity if we include what DeMark refers to as the TD Tolerance Level. The upside TD Tolerance Level multiplies the previous price bar's true range by 15 percent and adds the result to the current price bar's open. The downside TD Tolerance Level multiplies the previous price bar's true range by 15 percent and subtracts the result from the current price bar's open.

If the market opens within the projected range and then dips below the downside TD Tolerance Level before the high exceeds the projected high, then it's likely that the market will close within the projected range (**Figure 9.2**).

If the market opens within the projected range, and the high trades above the projected high before the price trades below the projected low and the downside TD Tolerance Level, it is likely that the market will close above the projected high (**Figure 9.3**).

If the market opens within the projected range and then moves above the upside TD Tolerance Level before the low exceeds the projected low, then it is likely that the market will close within the projected range.

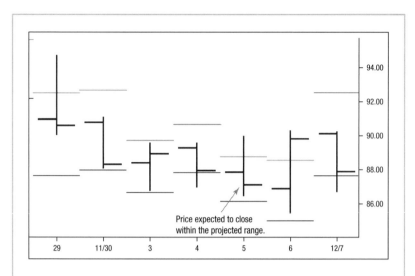

FIGURE 9.2   **TD Range Projection: Closing Back Within the Range**

In the daily chart of crude oil futures (WTI), price should close back within the projected range.

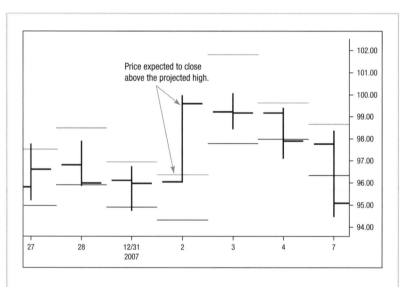

FIGURE 9.3   **TD Range Projection: Closing Above the Projected High**

In the daily chart of the crude oil future (WTI) above, price should close above the projected high.

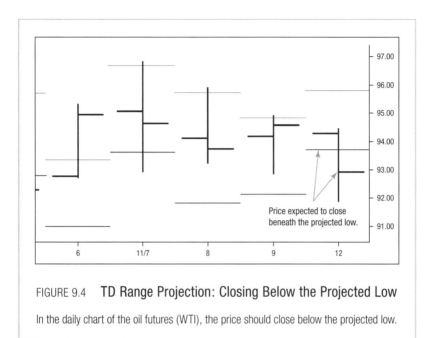

FIGURE 9.4   **TD Range Projection: Closing Below the Projected Low**

In the daily chart of the oil futures (WTI), the price should close below the projected low.

If the market opens within the projected range, and the low trades below the projected low before the price trades above the projected high and the upside TD Tolerance Level, it is likely that the market will close below the projected low (**Figure 9.4**).

TD Range Expansion Breakout (TD REBO)

The TD REBO is based on the notion that, when price breaks certain levels on an intrabar basis (see **Figures 9.5, 9.6, 9.7,** and **9.8**), it often acts as a precursor of further strength or weakness for the remainder of that price bar. Say, for example, that the market has been confined to a tight range for a while. If it then violates a fixed percentage of that range, an extended breakout is likely. TD REBO attempts to identify that initial price break, to enable traders to participate in the move, until a signal occurs in the opposite direction. The user chooses a predefined number of bars and the percentage value, but the structure itself is clear. Furthermore, if qualifiers are incorporated into the basic approach, the study can be used as a countertrend indicator, to buy weakness and sell strength. Although it would make more sense to combine TD REBO

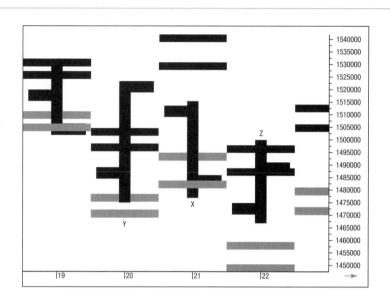

FIGURE 9.5   TD Range Expansion Breakout (REBO): Expectation for an Extended Up Move

In the daily chart of the Nikkei 225 (basis cash), the close of price bar X is lower than the close of price bar Y. Consequently, when the market trades above bar Z's open + (the range of bar X × 0.382), the expectation is for an extended up move toward bar Z's open + (the range of bar X × 0.618).

Source: CQG, Inc. © 2008. All rights reserved worldwide. www.cqg.com.

with other TD indicators to confirm the signals than to rely on TD REBO in isolation, this strategy is useful nonetheless and can be used either to generate entry points or to provide stops.

My preference is to apply TD REBO to daily price bars and use the current price bar's open as the base.

■ To Apply TD REBO to Daily Price Bars and Use the Current Price Bar's Open as the Base

First,

Multiply the previous day's true range separately by 0.382 and by 0.618.

Then

To calculate upside levels,

Add those values to the current day's opening price.

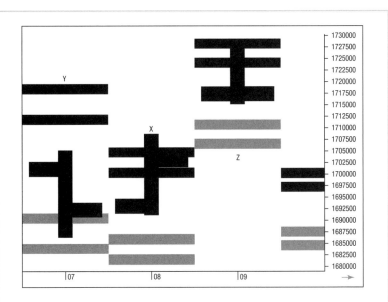

FIGURE 9.6   **TD Range Expansion Breakout (REBO): Expectation for a Near-Term Upside Price Exhaustion**

In the daily chart of the Nikkei 225 (basis cash), the close of price bar X is above the close of price bar Y. Consequently, when the market reaches bar Z's open + (the range of bar X × 0.618), the expectation is for near-term upside price exhaustion.

Source: CQG, Inc. © 2008. All rights reserved worldwide. www.cqg.com.

To determine downside levels,

Subtract them from the current day's opening price.

Using the qualifiers DeMark recommends for qualifying TD Line breaks, you can isolate instances in which, if the market breaks the first upside level, it is likely to reach the second upside level on an intraday basis. For example, if yesterday's close was a down close compared with the previous day's close, and then price takes out yesterday's true range multiplied by 0.382 and added to today's open, there's a good chance the up move will extend higher toward yesterday's true range multiplied by 0.618 and added to today's open on an intraday basis.

Conversely, if yesterday's close was an up close compared with the previous day's close, and then price takes out yesterday's true range multiplied by 0.382 and added to today's open, I'd be inclined to fade the market, and go short on an intraday basis if it reaches yesterday's true range multiplied by 0.618 and added to today's open.

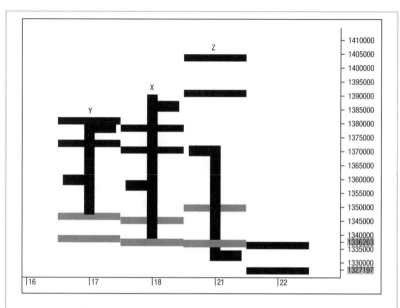

FIGURE 9.7   TD Range Expansion Breakout (REBO): Expectation for an
Extended Down Move

In the daily chart of the Nikkei 225 (basis cash), the close of price bar X is higher than
the close of price bar Y. Consequently, when the market trades below bar Z's open – (the
range of bar Y × 0.382 of bar X), the expectation is for an extended down-move toward
bar Z's open – (the range of bar X × 0.618).

Source: CQG, Inc. © 2008. All rights reserved worldwide. www.cqg.com.

Similarly, if yesterday was an up close compared with the previous day's close, and then price takes out yesterday's true range multiplied by 0.382 subtracted from today's open, there's a good chance the down move will extend lower, on an intraday basis, toward yesterday's true range multiplied by 0.618 and subtracted from today's open.

Conversely, if yesterday's close was a down close compared with the previous day's close, and then price takes out yesterday's true range multiplied by 0.382 and subtracted from today's open, I'd be inclined to fade the market and go long on an intraday basis if price reaches yesterday's true range multiplied by 0.618 and subtracted from today's open.

TD Channels

I've always found the concept of price channels interesting, but many of the traditional approaches to channel construction incorporate the

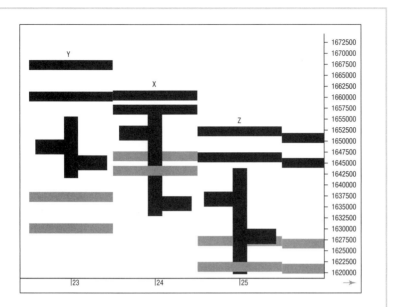

FIGURE 9.8   **TD Range Expansion Breakout (REBO): Expectation for a Near-Term Downside Price Exhaustion**

In the daily chart of the Nikkei 225 (basis cash) above, the close of price bar X is below the close of price bar Y. Consequently, when the market reaches bar Z's open – (the range of bar X × 0.618), the expectation is for near-term downside price exhaustion.

Source: CQG, Inc. © 2008. All rights reserved worldwide. www.cqg.com.

current price bar in their calculations, and their output is then suspect. Consequently, it is frustrating each time the market posts a new high or low, because this means the goalposts are continuously shifting on an intrabar basis. DeMark developed TD Channel I and TD Channel II to address this perceived problem.

TD Channel I. The construction of TD Channel I may seem counterintuitive, since a percentage multiplied by a series of lows is used to arrive at the upper channel, and a percentage multiplied by a series of highs is used to determine the lower channel.

■ **TD Channel I**

(For Currencies, Commodities, and Futures Markets)

To calculate the upper-channel boundary,

Multiply a three-bar moving average of the lows by 1.03.

To calculate the lower-channel boundary,

Multiply a three-bar moving average of the highs by 0.97.

Note that, while the current price bar is used in the calculation, the projected upper channel remains constant when prices are moving higher, while the projected lower level remains constant when the market pushes downward. DeMark recommends expanding the ratio multipliers to 91 percent and 109 percent when looking at single stocks.

More often than not, when prices are range bound, the market will be contained within the confines of TD Channel I, but a break of either the upper or the lower levels tends to coincide with market exhaustion. The channel extremes tend to be less effective when markets are trending, but they still provide some value, helping to isolate levels that would help initiate near-term price reversals. When the market closes outside the channel (**Figures 9.9** and **9.10**), it is often a short-term sign that the established trend is vulnerable, particularly if accompanied by a trend-exhaustion signal such as a TD Sequential or TD Combo signal.

TD Channel II. Unlike the less-orthodox, contemporary indicator TD Channel I, TD Channel II is calculated in a more-conventional manner.

■ TD Channel II

To determine the upper-channel boundary,

Multiply a three-bar moving average of the highs (including the current price bar) by 0.995.

To identify the lower-channel boundary,

Multiply a three-bar moving average of the lows (including the current price bar) by 1.005.

For single stocks,

Use a ratio of 0.930 or 1.070.

Price excursions outside of either the upper- or lower-channel boundary (**Figures 9.11** and **9.12**) are often associated with near-term trend exhaustion. In this instance, two consecutive closes in the same direction outside the channel boundaries often coincide with a short-term correction.

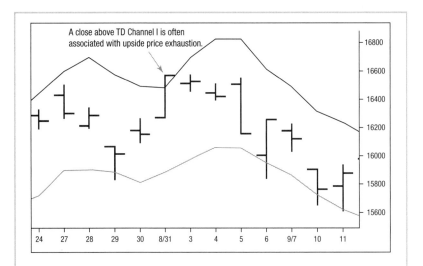

FIGURE 9.9　TD Channel I: How the Market Reverses

In the daily chart of the Nikkei 225 (basis cash), price is more often than not contained within the boundaries of the upper and lower channels, but note how the market reverses course following a close above the upper channel extreme.

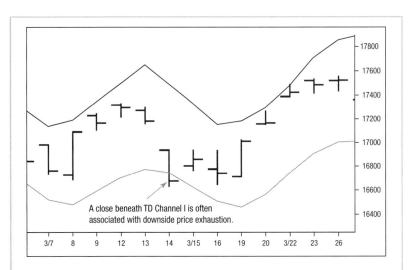

FIGURE 9.10　TD Channel I: How the Market Corrects

In the daily chart of the Nikkei 225 (basis cash), price is more often than not contained within the boundaries of the upper and lower channels, but note how the market corrects higher following a close beneath the lower channel extreme.

163

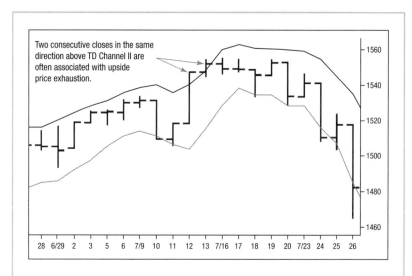

FIGURE 9.11 **TD Channel II: The Market Correcting Lower**

In the daily chart of the S&P 500 (basis cash), note how, after two consecutive closes above TD Channel II, the market corrects lower.

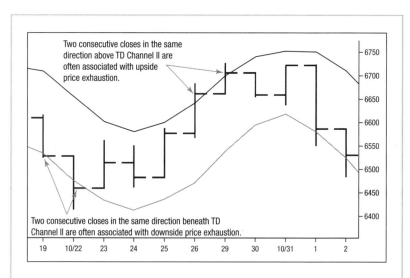

FIGURE 9.12 **TD Channel II: The Market Correcting Lower (Again)**

In the daily chart of the FTSE 100 (basis cash), note how, after two consecutive closes below TD Channel II, the market corrects higher, and, after two consecutive closes above TD Channel II, the market corrects lower.

CHAPTER 10

Short-Term Indicators
TD Differential,
TD Reverse Differential,
and TD Anti-Differential

THE INDICATORS in this chapter are for identifying price patterns on a short-term basis.

TD Differential

TD Differential attempts to compare buying and selling pressure over a two-bar horizon. Buying pressure is defined as the difference between the close of the current price bar and its true low (the true low is the lesser of either the current bar's low or the previous price bar's close); selling pressure is represented by the difference between the close of the current bar and its true high (the true high is the greater of the current price bar's high or the previous price bar's close).

When an up arrow appears after a TD Differential study is applied (**Figure 10.1**), it suggests that the high of the next price bar will be greater than the high of the current price bar, or at the very least, that the next price bar's close will be above the current price bar's close.

■ Conditions Necessary to Produce a TD Differential Up Arrow

The following are the conditions necessary to produce an up arrow:

1. There must be two consecutive closes, each one less than the one prior,

2. Buying pressure for the current price bar must exceed buying pressure from the previous price bar, and

3. Selling pressure for the current price bar must be less than selling pressure from the previous price bar.

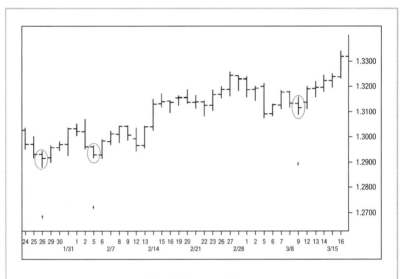

FIGURE 10.1   A Series of TD Differential Up Arrows

The daily chart of EURUSD depicts a series of TD Differential Up arrows. In each instance, the market meets all three of the following conditions: 1) There are two consecutive closes, each one less than the one prior; 2) buying pressure for the price bar marked with the arrow exceeds buying pressure from the previous price bar; and 3) selling pressure for the price bar marked with the arrow is less than selling pressure from the previous price bar.

When a down arrow appears after a TD Differential study is applied (**Figure 10.2**), it suggests the low of the next price bar will be less than the low of the current price bar, or at the very least, the next price bar's close will be beneath the current price bar's close.

■ Conditions Necessary to Produce a TD Differential Down Arrow

The following are the conditions necessary to produce a down arrow:

1. There must be two consecutive closes, each one greater than the one prior,

2. Selling pressure for the current price bar must exceed selling pressure from the previous price bar, and

3. Buying pressure for the current price bar must be less than buying pressure from the previous price bar.

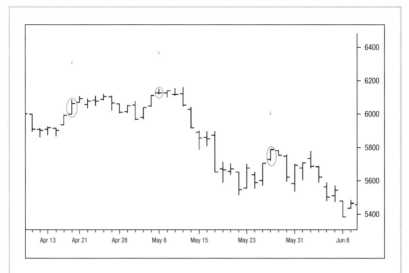

FIGURE 10.2 **A Series of TD Differential Down Arrows**

The daily chart of the German Dax (basis cash) depicts a series of TD Differential Down arrows. In each instance, the market meets all three of the following conditions: 1) There are two consecutive closes, each one greater than one prior; 2) selling pressure for the price bar marked with the arrow exceeds selling pressure from the previous price bar; and 3) buying pressure for the price bar marked with the arrow is less than buying pressure from the previous price bar.

TD Reverse Differential

TD Reverse Differential is similar to TD Differential, in the sense that it tries to measure buying and selling pressure to determine future price movements, but, whereas TD Differential is a near-term trend-reversal pattern, TD Reverse Differential is a near-term trend-continuation pattern (see **Figures 10.3** and **10.4**).

■ Conditions Necessary to Produce a TD Reverse Differential Down Arrow

1. There must be two consecutive closes, each one less than the prior close,

2. The current price bar's buying pressure must be less than the previous price bar's buying pressure, and

3. The current price bar's selling pressure must be greater than the previous bar's selling pressure.

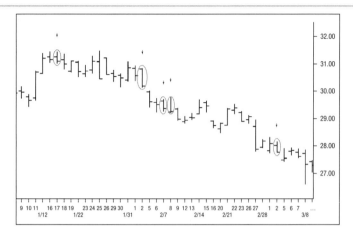

FIGURE 10.3 **A Series of TD Reverse Differential Down Arrows**

The daily chart of Microsoft depicts a series of TD Reverse Differential Down arrows. In each instance, the market meets all of the following conditions: 1) There are two consecutive lower closes, each one less than the prior close; 2) selling pressure for the price bar marked with the down arrow is greater than the previous price bar's selling pressure; and 3) buying pressure for the price bar marked with a down arrow is less than the previous bar's buying pressure.

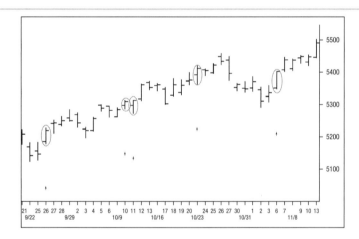

FIGURE 10.4 **A Series of TD Reverse Differential Up Arrows**

The daily chart of the CAC 40 (basis cash) depicts a series of TD Reverse Differential Up arrows. In each instance, the market meets all of the following conditions: 1) There are two consecutive higher closes, each one greater than the prior close; 2) buying pressure for the price bar marked with the up arrow is greater than the previous price bar's buying pressure; and 3) selling pressure for the price bar marked with an up arrow is less than the previous bar's selling pressure.

▦ Conditions Necessary to Produce a TD Reverse Differential Up Arrow

The following conditions are necessary to produce a TD Reverse Differential up arrow:

1. There must two consecutive higher closes, each one above the prior close,

2. The current price bar's buying pressure must be greater than the previous price bar's buying pressure, and

3. The selling pressure for the current price bar is less than the selling pressure for the previous bar.

TD Anti-Differential Up Arrow

Heading into a prospective market bottom, three conditions must be satisfied to generate a TD Anti–Differential up arrow (**Figure 10.5**).

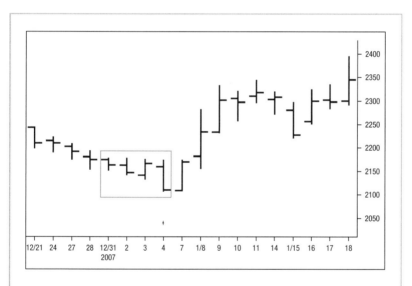

FIGURE 10.5 **A Prospective Market Bottom Suggested by the TD Anti-Differential Up Arrow**

The daily chart of Astrazeneca depicts a prospective market bottom suggested by the TD Anti-Differential up arrow: 1) There are two consecutive lower closes each (relative to the previous price bar's close), followed by 2) a higher close relative to the close of the previous price bar, and 3) a down close relative to the close of the previous price bar.

Conditions Necessary to Generate a TD Anti-Differential Up Arrow

To generate a TD Anti-Differential up arrow, there must be:

1. Two consecutive closes, each of which is lower relative to the previous price bar's close, followed by

2. A higher close relative to the close of the previous price bar, and then

3. A down close relative to the close of the previous price bar.

TD Anti-Differential Down Arrow

Heading into a prospective market top, three conditions must be satisfied to generate a TD Anti-Differential down arrow (**Figure 10.6**).

Conditions Necessary to Generate a TD Anti-Differential Down Arrow

To generate a TD Anti-Differential down arrow, there must be:

1. Two consecutive higher closes, each of which is higher relative to the previous price bar's close, followed by

2. A close that is lower than the close of the previous price bar, and then

3. A close that is higher relative to the close of the previous price bar.

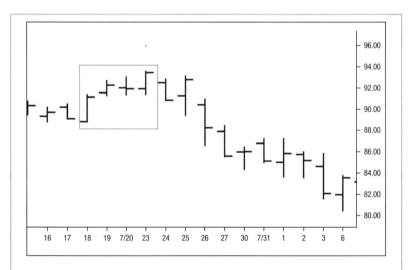

FIGURE 10.6   **A Prospective Market Top Suggested by the TD Anti-Differential Down Arrow**

The daily chart of Exxon Mobil depicts a prospective market top suggested by the TD Anti-Differential down arrow: 1) There are two consecutive closes, each of which is higher relative to the previous price bar's close, followed by 2) a close that is lower than the close of the previous price bar, and 3) a close that is higher relative to the close of the previous price bar.

CHAPTER 11

TD Waldo Patterns

At about the time Tom DeMark published his first book, *The New Science of Technical Analysis,* I was helping to organize a charity event in my spare time, a cartoon auction, at Christie's in London. The fundraising committee and I were really excited when we heard that the world-renowned author and artist Martin Handford had agreed to donate original artwork from one of his *Where's Wally?* books.

The *Where's Wally?* cartoons (as they are called in the U.K.), or *Where's Waldo?* (as they are known in the States), depict busy crowd scenes, often containing hundreds of different characters. The challenge for the reader is to find Wally, in his round glasses, striped bobble hat, and T-shirt, who is hidden somewhere amid the hustle and bustle.

I was amused, therefore, when Tom DeMark's book presented a series of price relationships that he referred to as *TD Waldo Patterns.* In much the same way that you can find the cartoon character if you look closely enough, you can find meaningful patterns if you carefully inspect a price chart, argues DeMark. He discovered a total of seven chart patterns, which he numbered two to eight (don't ask me what happened to number one). As with many of the TD indicators, you can apply these patterns to any market or time frame.

▪ TD Waldo Pattern Two

A prospective reversal bar can be identified when:

1. The market records a fresh high or low for a move, but closes higher than the four previous closes (for a potential base);

Or

2. The market closes lower than the four previous closes (for a potential top);

Or

3. The close of the trend high is greater than the previous price bar, or the close of the trend low is less than or equal to the previous price bar;

And

A down close occurs after a high or an up close occurs after a low, and the close following the high is greater than the close prior to the high, or the close following the low is less than the close prior to the low.

■ TD Waldo Pattern Three

First,

Identify price bars that have a range twice the range of the previous price bar.

To identify near-term upside exhaustion,

Add that value to the close of that bar.

To identify near-term downside price exhaustion,

Subtract the value from the close of the previous bar.

In addition,

If the market is advancing,

The high of the previous price bar must be above the high two price bars earlier.

If the market is declining,

The low of the previous price bar must be below the low two price bars earlier.

Moves such as these are often associated with short-term retardation of a trend or, at the very least, consolidation following a period of strength or weakness.

Note: An alternative, less-conservative option is simply to double the range of the previous price bar.

■ TD Waldo Pattern Four for a Prospective Bottom

TD Waldo Pattern Four looks for a situation in which:

1. The lowest price (X) was posted at least ten bars previously, and

2. Prior to that low, all prior lows were higher.

If

The next two price bars are below X, and both have lower closes than the close of the previous bar close,

Then

There's a reasonable chance that the down move is exhausted, and prices are predisposed to rally.

Note: This second close represents the TD Waldo pattern bar.

TD Waldo Pattern Four for a Prospective Top

TD Waldo Pattern Four looks for a situation in which:

The highest price (X) was posted at least ten bars previously, and, prior to that high, all prior highs were lower.

If

The next two price bars are above X, and both have higher closes than the close of the previous bar,

Then

There's a reasonable chance that the up move is exhausted near term, and prices are predisposed to decline.

Note: This second close represents the TD Waldo bar.

TD Waldo Pattern Five for a Prospective Top

1. The current bar's close should be equal to the close of the previous price bar, and
2. The close of the previous bar should be higher than the close of the bar before that.

TD Waldo Pattern Five for a Prospective Bottom

1. The close of the current bar should be equal to the close of the previous price bar, and
2. The previous bar's close should be lower than the close of the bar before that.

TD Waldo Pattern Six for a Prospective Bottom

If

1. The low of bar X is lower than all eight prior lows, and
2. The difference between the close and low of bar X is *greater than* the difference between the close and the low of the previous bar,

Then

Bar X qualifies as the start of a potential upside reversal.

■ TD Waldo Pattern Six for a Prospective Top

If

1. The high of bar X is higher than all eight prior highs, and
2. The difference between the close and high of bar X is greater than the difference between the close and high of the previous bar,

Then

Bar X qualifies as the start of a potential downside reversal.

TD Waldo Pattern Seven combines both a reference price level and a time condition to identify a prospective short-term trend reversal.

■ TD Waldo Pattern Seven for a Prospective Short-Term Reversal

For a Potential Bottom:

The market must close above the close four bars prior to a TD Point low (that is, a low flanked by a higher low to its immediate left and to its immediate right).

For a Potential Top:

The market must close below the close four bars prior to a TD Point high (that is, a high flanked by a lower high to its immediate left and to its immediate right).

■ TD Waldo Pattern Eight

For a Potential Short-Term Top:

The close of the current price bar must be *higher* than all seven prior highs, but *lower* than the close five bars earlier.

For a Potential Bottom:

The close of the current price bar must be *lower* than all seven prior lows, but *higher* than the close five bars earlier.

CHAPTER 12

Putting It All Together

ONCE YOU HAVE LEARNED the DeMark studies and become proficient using them as standalone indicators, the real challenge is to apply them to real-time trading. Although I do not profess to know all the answers, and, after fourteen years, still find myself learning new things, what follows is an example of how I like to combine some of the DeMark indicators to get a macroinsight into what is going on in the market and how things might play out.

One example of a way to combine the indicators is to look at multiple time frames, as I did with the USD Index (DXY) of February 2007 (see **Figures 12.1–12.3**). The other example relates to the U.S. dollar vs. the Japanese yen (the USDJPY, **Figures 12.4–12.8**). A number of factors conspired to suggest that the market was about to base (that is, that the U.S. dollar would strengthen against the Japanese yen) towards the end of November 2007.

First, USDJPY came within a few pips of the TD D-Wave Five down projection at 107.17 (**Figure 12.4**). Interestingly, this level was very close to the midpoint of the 0.8919 and 0.8423 downside TD Trend Factor levels at 107.61 and the TD Magnet Price of the TD Retracement Arc at 106.98 from June 22, 2007 (**Figure 12.5**). The low in USDJPY was also in the same vicinity as the 0.764 Fibonacci retracement of the January 2005 to mid-June 2007 advance at 106.99, and the downside TD Propulsion target at 107.34 (**Figure 12.6**). At the same time, the market completed a TD Combo Buy (Version II) and a TD Aggressive Combo Buy (**Figure 12.7**), while more conventional

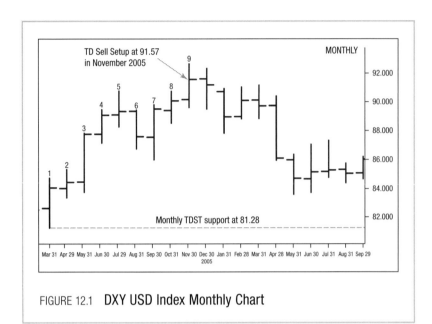

FIGURE 12.1 **DXY USD Index Monthly Chart**

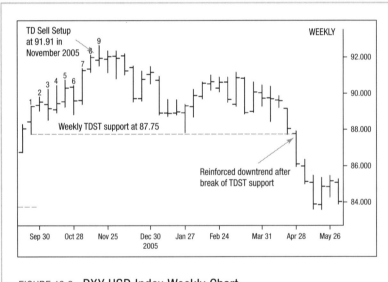

FIGURE 12.2 **DXY USD Index Weekly Chart**

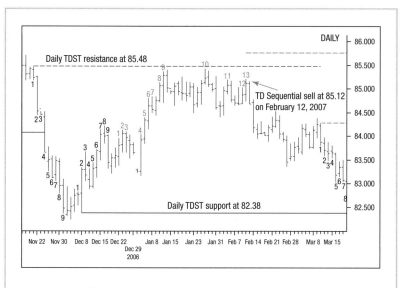

FIGURE 12.3 DXY Dollar Index Daily Chart

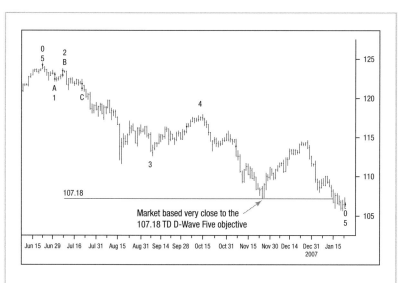

FIGURE 12.4 USDJPY Daily Chart with TD D-Wave

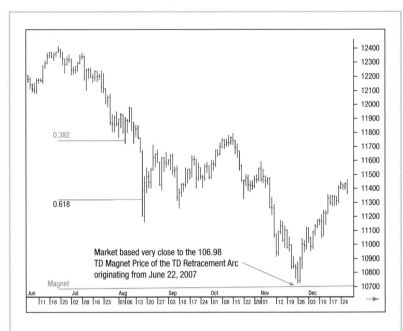

FIGURE 12.5 **USDJPY Daily Chart with TD Retracement Arc**

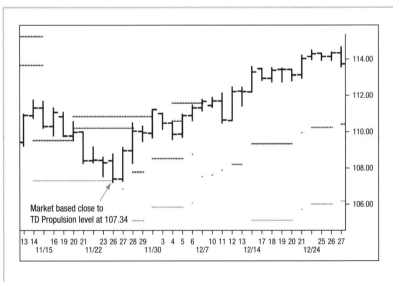

FIGURE 12.6 **USDJPY Daily Chart with TD Propulsion**

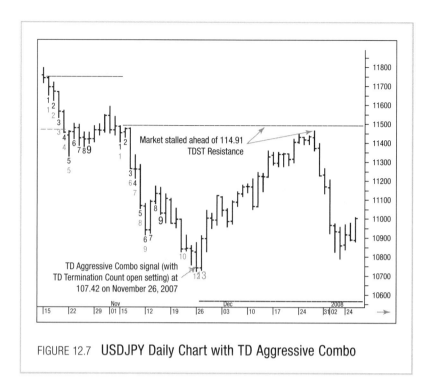

FIGURE 12.7 **USDJPY Daily Chart with TD Aggressive Combo**

technical analysis would have shown a bullish, engulfing candlestick pattern (where the open-close range on November 26, 2007, exceeded the open-close range on November 26).

At the same time, the BKX Index (the KBW Bank Index) generated a TD Sequential Buy signal, and the UBS FX Risk Index (see sidebar for its components) produced a TD Sequential Sell signal (**Figure 12.8**).

■ The UBS FX Risk Index Components

i/ii. Currency volatility,

iii. The VIX Index,

iv. Gold, priced in euros and U.S. dollars,

v. Performance of stocks relative to U.S. Treasuries on a monthly basis,

vi. Spreads between high yields and U.S. Treasuries,

vii. Spreads between the JPM (J. P. Morgan) EMBI + emerging markets index and the U.S. Treasury curve,

viii. The monthly performance of utility stocks relative to S&P 500 financials.

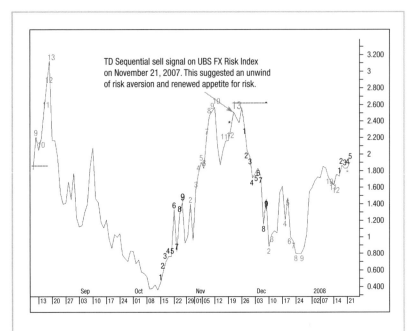

FIGURE 12.8 **UBS FX Risk Index: Daily Chart with TD Sequential**

Source: CQG, Inc. All rights reserved worldwide. www.cqg.com. Data from UBS AG

Although it is somewhat counterintuitive, a rising index suggests that investors are becoming risk averse, and a declining index suggests investors are becoming risk seeking. In the example above, it was significant that the index had an active sell signal at the end of November 2007, which implied renewed interest in carry trades (one of which was a bullish USDJPY).

The USDJPY buy signal was further reinforced when it generated a TD Price Flip on the close of November 27 (that is, a close above the close four price bars earlier) and satisfied the conditions for a TD Reference close on November 28 (when the market traded above the highest close within the four price bars prior to the low on November 26). Interestingly, the ensuing recovery, which was arguably a TD D-Wave I up, stalled ahead of 114.91 daily TDST resistance (the absolute price high of the TD Setup that began on November 5, 2007).

CHAPTER 13

Learning the DeMark Indicators

I'M OFTEN ASKED what is the easiest way to learn the DeMark indicators. Fortunately, it's considerably easier now than when I first started. (I'm not looking for sympathy—I'm glad I found out about them when I did because it meant I had a head start and could learn them firsthand from Tom.) All I had to go on then was DeMark's first book, *The New Science of Technical Analysis* (Wiley, 1994), which had some great ideas but was hard to follow, because his work wasn't available in any of the mainstream market-information systems at the time.

It's all very different now. Tom wrote another two books, *New Market Timing Techniques* (Wiley, 1997) and *DeMark on Day Trading Options* (McGraw-Hill, 1999), and the DeMark indicators are now readily available on the Bloomberg Professional service, and on Aspen Graphics, CQG, Thomson Financial, and TradeStation software. The help guides on each of these market-data platforms are excellent. Each has its respective merits but, for educational purposes, the Bloomberg has some particularly good learning aids, notably TD Cursor Commentary, which enables the user to click on a price bar, apply a data cursor, and see an interpretation based on the DeMark studies applied to that chart. There's even a live instant-messaging service, TD Chat, in which Tom DeMark participates, to provide active educational insight into the real-time market application of his studies. Finally, once you're familiar with the DeMark indicators, it's worth taking a look at TD Re-Search (TDRS), a scan facility that enables users to search the Bloomberg for DeMark indicator–based signals on daily, weekly, and monthly time frames. All these services are being continually improved and refined, to keep up with Tom DeMark's development of his indicators.

■ Using TD Cursor Commentary

1. Launch a price chart.

2. Apply whichever DeMark indicators you want to use.

3. Then, click on the gray Commentary button.

Now you will be able to use your mouse to move the cursor to the bar you want to analyze. If you click on that bar, a pop-up window appears, providing a summary page that explains the indicator construction, its current indications, and its implications for the future.

FIGURE 13.1 **EURCAD Daily Chart with TD Sequential**

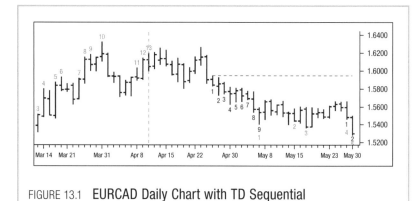

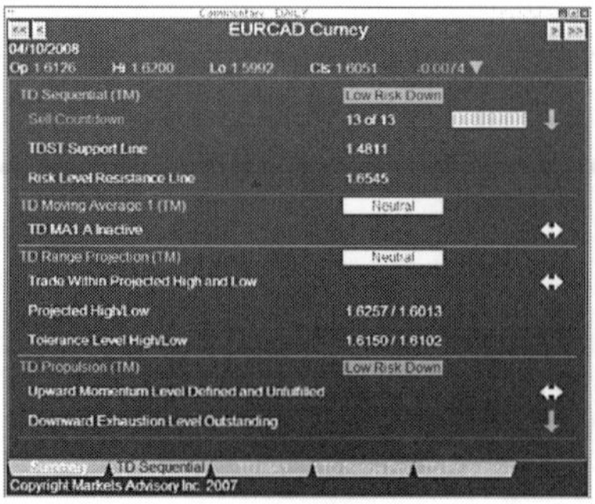

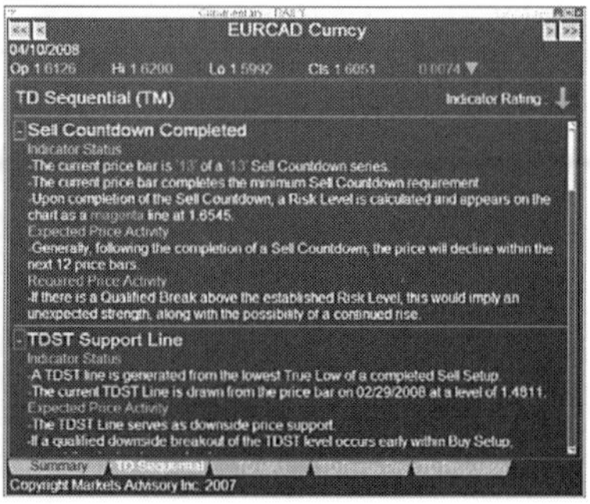

FIGURE 13.2 AND FIGURE 13.3 **EURCAD Currency Analyses**

TDRS <GO> enables you to scan equities, equity options, credit and fixed-income markets, ETFs, currencies, futures, and commodities.

Below are instructions that will allow you to access the service (provided by Markets Advisory, which is Tom DeMark's company).

TDRS <GO>

Type TDRS <GO>, and select your search criteria:

Indicator lists the various DeMark studies that your scans can be based on.

Time allows you to select from daily, weekly, or monthly (with intraday to be added soon).

Asset/Portfolio allows you to select from:

• A user-defined custom portfolio
• Active world markets
• Equities (subdivided by country, U.S. equity options, ETFs by region, world equity indexes, and credit-default swaps)
• Fixed income
• Futures and options on commodities
• Foreign exchange

Scan Output, under Symbols, shows the number of instruments in the chosen asset class. Double-click to view them in either alphabetical or chronological order, and you will be able to view the current and past four days' indicator readings.

Click on an individual instrument, and you'll have the option to launch a chart with your chosen TD indicator applied, and see an indicator overview and related news/research. The Spreadsheet View option is particularly useful; it displays snapshot indicator-reading overview on multiple time frames for a number of TD studies.

In addition to the TD Chat, users can also contact the following Bloomberg applications specialists for assistance:

Asia   Gregg Tan, greggtan@bloomberg.net

Europe   Guido Riolo, guidoriolo@bloomberg.net

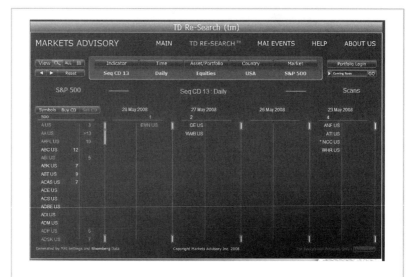

FIGURE 13.4 TD Re-Search Screen

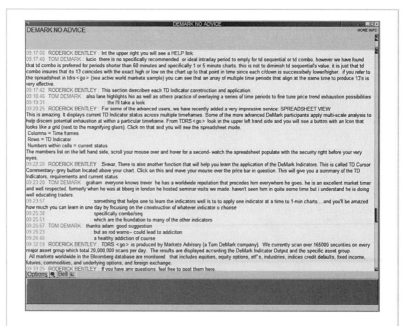

FIGURE 13.5 DeMark IB Chat Screen

The screen above is an interaction between Tom DeMark and Bloomberg product spe-
cialist Rod Bentley. Tom and Rod participate actively on TD Chat's *DeMark No Advice*,
answering questions about the practical application of the indicators. The chat is available
to all Bloomberg users upon request.

North America   Roderick Bentley, rbentley@bloomberg.net
                             Doug Tengler, dtengler1@bloomberg.net

Specific functionality questions should be addressed to either Eugene Sorenson, esorenson1@bloomberg.net, who developed the charting functionality at Bloomberg, or Rick Knox, rknox@capitalmarketsresearch .com, who developed the TDRS functionality to Tom's specifications. Stan Yabroff, at CQG, is also a fantastic resource.

Index

For the reader's ease of use, index entries are listed without the "TD" designation that is a part of the trademarked name of each TD indicator. This omission in no way is meant to imply that the name is to be used elsewhere without its full, trademarked appellation.

About Bloomberg

Bloomberg L.P., founded in 1981, is a global information services, news, and media company. Headquartered in New York, Bloomberg has sales and news operations worldwide.

Serving customers on six continents, Bloomberg, through its wholly-owned subsidiary Bloomberg Finance L.P., holds a unique position within the financial services industry by providing an unparalleled range of features in a single package known as the Bloomberg Professional® service. By addressing the demand for investment performance and efficiency through an exceptional combination of information, analytic, electronic trading, and straight-through-processing tools, Bloomberg has built a worldwide customer base of corporations, issuers, financial intermediaries, and institutional investors.

Bloomberg News, founded in 1990, provides stories and columns on business, general news, politics, and sports to leading newspapers and magazines throughout the world. Bloomberg Television, a 24-hour business and financial news network, is produced and distributed globally in seven languages. Bloomberg Radio is an international radio network anchored by flagship station Bloomberg 1130 (WBBR-AM) in New York.

In addition to the Bloomberg Press line of books, Bloomberg publishes *Bloomberg Markets* magazine.

To learn more about Bloomberg, call a sales representative at:

London: +44-20-7330-7500
New York: +1-212-318-2000
Tokyo: +81-3-3201-8900

About the Author

Jason Perl is global head of Fixed Income, Currencies & Commodities Technical Strategy at UBS Investment Bank. He joined UBS's FX Technical Strategy Group in London in July 2000, and has been running the group since 2004.

Prior to joining UBS, he was an independent consultant in several areas: advising proprietary desks and hedge funds on short-term trading strategies, helping institutional investors with trading-system design and development, and acting as technical strategy adviser to a number of large financial data vendors and as contributing editor for *Futures & Options World*, *FX&MM*, and the International Petroleum Exchange's (IPE) *Pipeline* magazine.

Perl's area of technical expertise is the DeMark indicators, which he has been using for the past fourteen years. In his current role, he and his team provide both short- and medium-term trading strategies to central banks, hedge funds, institutional investors, and wealth managers around the world; and general, specialist-education technical-analysis training.

Robin Hood Foundation

A portion of the advance received by the author for this book goes to the Robin Hood Foundation. Robin Hood changes fates and saves lives in New York City by applying investment principles to charitable giving and supporting the most effective poverty-fighting programs in all five boroughs. Go to www.robinhood.org.